VINTAGE KNIT

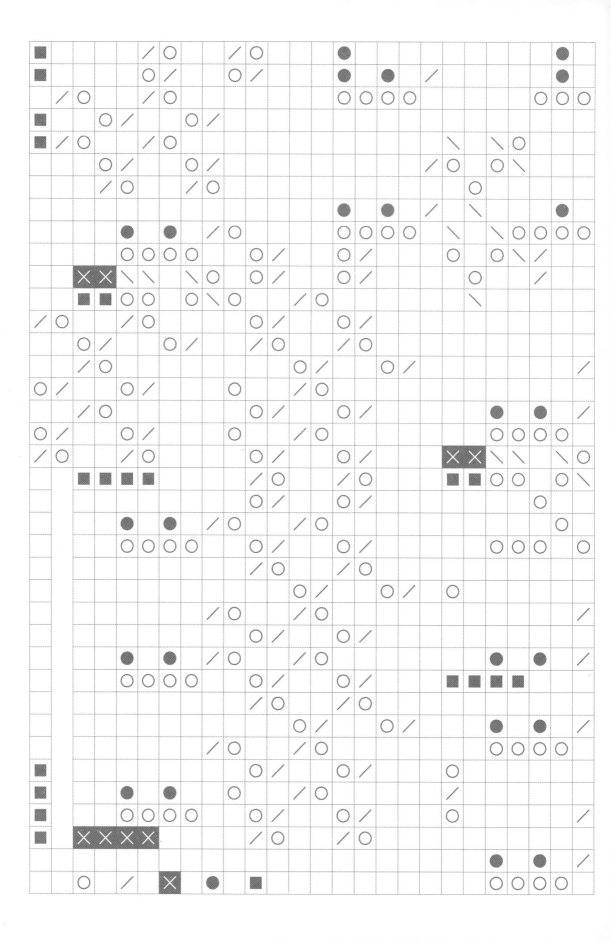

MARINE MALAK
WITH GERALDINE WARNER

VINTAGE KNIT

25 KNITTING & CROCHET PATTERNS
REFASHIONED FOR TODAY

LAURENCE KING PUBLISHING

LAURENCE KING

Published in 2014 by Laurence King Publishing Ltd
361–373 City Road
London EC1V 1LR
United Kingdom
Tel: +44 20 7841 6900
Fax: +44 20 7841 6910
E-mail: enquiries@laurenceking.com
www.laurenceking.com

ISBN: 978-1-78067-166-6

Design and original concept by Marine Malak.
Additional text, pattern grading and technical advice
by Geraldine Warner.

Photograph on front jacket reproduced with permission of Hearst
Communication Inc.
Artwork on frontispiece and hard cover by Simon Hughes.

Photography by Simon Pask except: pp.13–15, 25–26, 29, 31, 89 & 92
by Marine Malak and Alex Madjitey.

Make-up by Karen Fundell except: pp.13–15, 25–26, 29, 31, 89 & 92
by Salma Salama.

Models: Emma Gojkovic, Georgia Gideon, Jade Impleton-Jackman,
Alya Mooro and Lana Al-Mulla.

Knitters: Julia Bishop, Annie Christopher, Vanessa Hubbard,
Jean Jeakins, Jean Luff and Lisa Williamson.

Garment diagrams: Geraldine Warner.

Picture research: Heather Vickers.
Printed in China

CONTENTS

INTRODUCTION

When I was approached to co-author this project I was thrilled: here was something that coincided with my own thoughts on 'vintage' knitting. This book proves that hand-made knitwear can be relevant, youthful, fun and stylish. Shot in a modern context, it's aimed at a new generation of knitters who are looking for something stylish to suit them, a reason to find hand-knitting fresh and exciting, despite the age of the original patterns.

Let's start with the term 'vintage'. It has become a popular, all-encompassing movement that, at its core, covers approximately 60 years of the 20th century, from 1920 to 1980 (although purists stop at the 1960s). It defines any visual arts from that period, encompassing fashion, textiles, art, craft and homeware. The web means that we are able to cherry-pick our influences — fashion has never been so accessible or so easy to source, meaning that we're less hung up on what's fashionable, and more interested in individual expression. This is good news for knitting — let's face it, the creation of a knitted garment isn't the quickest process in the world and in the past there's been the risk of knitting something that is 'on-trend' this season, only to find it's 'out' by the time you've finished it!

Fashion, as we know, is an ever-changing beast but, on the whole, the way in which garments are made doesn't stray too far from the basics. Of course there have been technical innovations meaning that the method is often taken out of our own hands and given to machines, or the foundation materials themselves have changed, but the fundamental methods of creating fabric and putting together home-made garments remain the same.

This is particularly true of hand-knitting, a craft which, essentially, has not changed over the last 100 years. Its popularity has gone through peaks and troughs, and its context has altered over time (historical events, sociological changes and technological innovations have seen to that), but it's still with us and is currently undergoing a revival. The spirit of experimentation is with us again, at least in terms of techniques, and it's during a surge like this current one that we can also afford to look at ways of taking the craft forward.

So what do we take with us from this period of looking back? Rather than relegating this 'vintage revival' to the past, fossilizing it along with its influences, what do we pack in our suitcase to take with us on the next part of the journey? For me one of the most interesting elements of mid-20th-century knitting is the way it was allied so closely to the fashion of the time, and yet the quality and style give the designs an everlasting longevity. The finer yarns and needles used during that period meant that tailored details that emulated woven fabric were possible, plus a wider knowledge of crochet and sewing meant that these elements in a knitting pattern were not as off-putting as they might seem to some knitters today. Of course, clothing production has altered so much since that time, and the cost has dropped considerably, resulting in hand-knitting becoming a luxury rather than a necessity, but that doesn't mean to say we have to lose the possibilities. The potential is there to adapt our expectations and remind ourselves what knitting can do.

Since knitting is no longer regarded as a necessity, the amount of time we are willing to spend on it has dwindled: we look for quick-to-knit projects and that usually means thicker yarns and needles, but is it possible we're missing out here? Why knit for the sake of it when you can discover a world of truly satisfying projects which, given a little extra time, produce unique and wearable garments that will reflect the style you're personally interested in?

So here we are; we've reached a point again where fashion and knitting have coincided and that, for me, is the thing to pack into our knitting travel bag. The original patterns in this book might have begun life 70 years ago, but the context and the craft itself are right now.

Geraldine Warner

HOW TO USE THIS BOOK

Vintage Knit is aimed at intermediate–advanced knitters, so although we have offered some method explanations, we expect the knitter to bring some experience to the projects. Having said that, the main thing to anticipate when approaching an older pattern is often patience. Expect to spend more time on the project than you might on a modern design that uses larger needles and thicker yarn.

We have covered a range of projects in simplicity and size, ranging from Easy (1 out of 5) to Difficult (5 out of 5). As well as technique and stitch, the difficulty level can sometimes be a reflection of the time and patience spent on a certain stitch or even the sheer volume of the knitting (see the Charming Dress and Fashionable Housecoat).

Many of the projects use crochet in one form or another, either as a main stitch (Blouse Front and Book Bag), an accessory (the scarf in Spiral Pattern Jumper), buttons (Twinset in Simple Stitches), or simply as a way of firming up a border or adding button loops. We have used basic crochet stitches, but if you are not confident with crochet, we have covered the techniques used in the patterns in the 'Methods' section on the next page.

The book is written using UK terminology for both knitting and crochet. We have included conversion tables of differences in UK and US terms on page 11 — if you're unsure, please familiarize yourself with these before starting a pattern.

METHODS

There are so many knitting techniques available to you that it's impossible to list all of them here (and that would be a different book!), but the stand-out topics we've listed below include some essentials that you can't get started (or finished) without. Feel free to explore other methods and, of course, to use your own preferred techniques.

BUTTONS AND BUTTON LOOPS

Crochet buttons and button loops are common features in vintage patterns. They create a unique touch, but the instructions on the original patterns usually expect the knitter to know how to create these features. The button loops especially are particularly easy and give you scope to create a loop to fit your chosen size of button.

TO MAKE A BUTTON LOOP
Start by working 1 row of dc (sc) along the edge of the work.

Insert hook through work from front to back where loop is desired and create a sl st. Make sufficient number of chains long enough to go around button. Attach the chain to the edge using a sl st.

Where knitted or crochet buttons are required, instructions are given in the individual pattern.

CROCHET

Most of the patterns in this book are knitted (except the Blouse Front and Book Bag), but many of them use crochet for accessories (Spiral Pattern Jumper), edging, buttons and button loops (see left) or for finishing. Instructions for edgings and adornments are given on each individual pattern.

Generally the crochet stitches used are straightforward and simple to work, but just to complicate matters the terms differ between the UK and US.

For clarification, the default abbreviations you see in the book take the UK terms as standard, while the US terms are in brackets. The list of crochet terms used with their UK/US equivalents can be found on page 11.

GRAFTING

Grafting (also known as weaving or kitchener stitch) is used to join two pieces of knitting together seamlessly. It is commonly employed when joining the end of sock toes together (which is where it is used in this book). The stitches to be grafted need to be left on the needle. The pieces are grafted from right to left, with each needle having the same number of stitches.

The following example uses Stocking stitch (used for the toes in the Trim Ankle Socks) as the primary stitch. Position your pieces by holding the needles parallel with the tips pointing in the same direction and the wrong sides facing each other. Thread a darning needle with the yarn tail from one of the pieces of knitting.

STEP 1
Insert sewing needle knitwise through first st on front knitting needle, draw yarn through and sl the st off the knitting needle.

STEP 2
Insert sewing needle purlwise through second st on front knitting needle, draw yarn through, leaving the st on the needle.

STEP 3
Insert sewing needle purlwise through the first st on back knitting needle, draw yarn through and sl the st off.

STEP 4
Insert sewing needle knitwise through the second st on back knitting needle, leaving the st on the needle.

Rep Steps 1–4.

CROCHET HOOK SIZES

Metric	US	UK Imperial
2mm	[n/a]	14
2.25mm	B/1	13
3mm	[n/a]	11
3.25mm	D/3	10
3.5mm	E/4	[n/a]
3.75mm	F/5	9
4mm	G/6	6

KNITTING NEEDLE SIZES

Metric	US
2mm	0
2.25mm	1
2.75mm	2
3mm	[n/a]
3.25mm	3
3.75mm	5
4mm	6
4.5mm	7
5mm	8
5.5mm	9

MAKING UP

Each pattern has its own directions concerning the construction of the garment, but we leave the specific methods chosen up to you. Having said that, here are some issues you might like to consider.

CASTING ON & OFF

There are many different casting on and off techniques, so please feel free to use your preferred method. For simplicity's sake we recommend a standard cable cast-on.

Create a slip-knot. Insert the right needle knitwise into the st on the left needle. Wrap the yarn round the right needle as if to knit. Draw the yarn through the first st to make a new st, but instead slip the new st to the left needle. Insert the right needle between the two sts on the left needle. Wrap the yarn around the right needle as if to knit and pull the yarn through to make a new st. Slip the new st to the left needle.

Again, for casting off we go for a basic knit cast-off method; however, when a rib stitch is used, the pattern instructions will direct the knitter to cast off ribwise.

SEAMS

This is another area where there are many methods available to the knitter, and your choice can make the difference between a professional and an amateur-looking finish. Very generally speaking, mattress stitch is recommended for side seams, whereas good old back-stitch gives a strength suitable for setting in sleeves.

Shoulders are another area that needs strength and give your garment a firm structure: the recommended method for seaming shoulders is an invisible 'knit' stitch.

SHOULDER SEAM 'KNIT' STITCH

Place both pieces of work flat with RS facing upwards and edges butting against each other (as for mattress stitch). You need to line up the pieces so that each stitch of the shoulder is facing the other. Insert sewing needle under a whole st inside the cast-off edge of one side, then under the corresponding st on the other side. Continue along the shoulder, matching st for st on each piece.

ALTERNATIVE SHOULDER SEAM METHODS

Keep the stitches 'live' (i.e. do not cast them off the needles) and either 'graft' them together (see 'Grafting' on page 8) for a less structured seam or, where shoulders are straight (i.e. not 'stepped'), you can use the 'Three-needle cast-off' technique for a slightly firmer seam, as follows.

THREE-NEEDLE CAST-OFF TECHNIQUE

Keeping the sts for both shoulders 'live', place both sides of work together with RS facing inwards (WS facing outwards). Hold both needles in your left hand and, with a third needle, knit the first 2 sts from both needles together. Repeat, then pull the first st over the second to cast off. Continue until all sts have been cast off.

If in doubt, use a back-stitch, but only as a last resort if you're really not sure how to work the previous methods!

BLOCKING

Knitters are often nervous about blocking: what's it for? How do you do it? Blocking is a method involving water or steam in order to gain a more even knitted surface. It's carried out on individual pieces before sewing up, and can also be used when you want to eke out a little bit more stretch from your fabric — particularly useful when you're working with negative ease. Before you think about blocking your knitted pieces, you'll need to check that the yarn you've used is suitable to go through the process. If so, first decide whether you want to steam or wet block.

Steam method

Pin out your pieces (before making up, obviously!) onto a blocking board (WS facing up), measuring the pieces as you go to make sure they match the desired dimensions, hold the iron approx 1in (2.5cm) above the fabric and hit the 'steam' button. Never allow the iron to touch the fabric. Allow to dry thoroughly before removing from the board. Do not block any ribbed areas.

Wet blocking method

This is a labour-intensive method and is really only necessary for fine, intricate items such as lace shawls. Dip the fabric into water, gently squeeze out the excess water, then gently pin out the pieces to the desired dimensions and leave to dry.

Natural wool will respond well to being pressed lightly on the WS using a warm iron over a damp cloth. Other yarns, for example silk, should not come into direct contact with heat, even through a damp cloth.

Check each pattern for details on how best to block or press your garment.

SHOULDER PADS

There are different ways to make shoulder pads. Here are two examples.

TRIANGULAR SHOULDER PAD

This method features heavily in vintage patterns and is a straightforward triangle, giving a more boxy look to the shoulder silhouette.

Materials: 1 pair 3.25mm (US #3) needles, a small amount of 4-ply yarn.
Tension: 7.5 sts & 9 rows = 1in (2.5cm)

Cast on 20 sts and work in St-st for 6in (15cm). Cast off. Fold in half diagonally and sew together leaving a small gap for stuffing. You can stuff using leftover yarn cut into short lengths, cotton wool or a sliver of wadding. Oversew gap and darn in all ends.

SHAPED SHOULDER PAD

This shape is more familiar to us today and creates a pad that moulds itself more to the shoulder.

Materials: 1 pair 3.25mm (US #3) needles, a small amount of 4-ply yarn.
Tension: 7.5 sts & 9 rows = 1in (2.5cm)

Cast on 3 sts. Working in garter-st, inc 1 st at each end of next and every following RS row until there are 21 sts, ending with a RS row. Mark the centre st.

Next row (dec row) (WS): K to within 1 st of centre st, sl this st and the centre st tog knitwise, k1, pass both sl sts over (p2sso), k to end.

Cont to inc at each end of every other row until there are 29 sts. Rep the dec row (27 sts). Inc each end of every other row until there are 33 sts. Rep the dec row (31 sts). Cast off loosely.

You can alter the thickness of the pad by using a single layer as it is, or you can make two the same and stitch them together. If you go for the latter, you can then either leave the layers as they are, or stuff them as for the Triangular Pad.

SIZING, FIT AND EASE

We're very used to wearing our modern garments with generous ease — that is to say, the amount of space between the clothing and your body. Modern ease can be anything from 2in (5cm) upwards, whereas many of the patterns in this book are intended to be very close-fitting like the original vintage designs and have zero ease, or sometimes even stray into negative ease; this means the measurements of the finished garment are smaller than the wearers'. This is intentional and will allow for the elasticity of the knitted fabric to stretch to your measurements (particularly where a predominantly ribbed stitch is used), so always follow the 'to fit sizes' measurements if you're trying to emulate the vintage fit.

When in doubt, check the 'Actual Finished Measurements' section of the pattern, which will tell you what the final fit will be.

TENSION/GAUGE

This is the section that most people skip, but which is actually the most important, particularly where close-fitting vintage patterns are concerned. You may be confident that your own tension is usually pretty close to the mark, but you should always make sure that it matches the guidelines in individual patterns — don't forget, you're working to the designer's own tension, which in turn will vary from pattern to pattern.

Each pattern has a tension/gauge guide that gives you a guide as to how many stitches and rows were worked to 1in (2.5cm) when the garment measurements were worked out. The guidelines are measured over 4in (10cm) and expect you to knit a swatch measuring the same. The instructions will also tell you which stitch was used to work up the swatch where more than one stitch is used in the pattern. Skip this step at your knitted peril!

WRAP AND TURN (W&T)

Some of the patterns in this book use short rows as a shaping method — this is where you work a number of stitches, then turn the work before you reach the end of the row. Worked over several rows this creates extra fabric in one area of the knitting (for example, bust darts or sock heels). If you turn your knitting without using the Wrap and Turn technique, a small hole will be visible where you've turned, so you'll need to follow the instructions below (assuming the main stitch used is Stocking stitch).

Row 1 (RS): K to the number of sts given in the pattern. 'Wrap' the next st as follows: sl the next st onto the right-hand needle purlwise. Bring the yarn between the needles to the front of the work. Transfer the st back to the left-hand needle. Turn the work so that the WS is facing.

Row 2: P to the number of sts given in the pattern. 'Wrap' the next st as above. Turn the work so that the RS is facing.

When you've completed your short rows and you come to knit across all the sts together, you'll need to make sure that you knit each wrapped st together with the strand of yarn (lying at the base of the wrapped st) you used to wrap it.

The Trim Ankle Socks use an alternative way of avoiding a hole, which was the method used in the original pattern. When it comes to knitting back over all the sts, you will reach a gap between each st omitted before turning — pick up the loop lying between the st just worked and that st, place it on the left-hand needle, then k2 tog. This is by no means an invisible method, but can be included in the design (it works rather nicely on the sock heel, for instance).

UK/US TERMINOLOGY

UK	US	Description
Cast off	Bind off	The last row of knitting, worked to remove the fabric from the needle.
Garter stitch (garter-st)	Plain	Knit every row.
Jumper	Sweater	The word 'jumper' is not used much outside the UK.
Moss stitch (moss-st)	Seed stitch	A textured st, created as follows: (k1, p1) to end of row. Alternate knitted and purled sts on following row.
Stocking stitch (St-st)	Stockinette stitch	K1 row, p1 row.
Tension	Gauge	A method of measuring how many sts and rows are worked to the inch or centimetre.

KNITTING ABBREVIATIONS

alt	alternate		p2 tog	purl two together
approx	approximately		p3 tog	purl three together
CC	contrasting colour		patt	pattern
cm	centimetres		psso	pass slipped stitch over
cont	continue		rem	remaining
dec	decrease		rep	repeat
dpn(s)	double-pointed needle(s)		rev St-st	reverse Stocking stitch
g	grams		rnd(s)	round(s)
garter-st	garter stitch		RS	right side
in	inches		sl	slip
inc	increase		sl 1	slip one stitch
k	knit		sl st	slip stitch
k2 tog	knit two together		st(s)	stitch(es)
k3 tog	knit three together		St-st	Stocking stitch
kfb	knit into front and back of next stitch		st-holder	stitch holder
m	metres		tbl	through back of loop
m1	make one		tog	together
MC	main colour		w&t	wrap and turn (see opposite)
mm	millimetres		WS	wrong side
moss-st	moss stitch		yb	bring yarn to back of work
p	purl		yf	bring yarn to front of work
p1f&b	purl one front and back		yrn	yarn round needle

CROCHET ABBREVIATIONS

ch	chain
dtr (trc)	double treble (triple crochet in US)
dc (sc)	double crochet (single crochet in US)
htr (hdc)	half treble (half double crochet in US)
sk	skip
sp	space
sl st	slip stitch
tr (dc)	treble crochet (double crochet in US)

ATTRACTIVE SKULL CAP
FOR CASUAL WEAR

MATERIALS
Handmaiden Casbah, 81% merino/
9% cashmere/10% nylon, 355yds
(325m) per 115g, as follows:

1 x 115g in Peach Blossom

1 pair 3.25mm (US #3) needles

SIZING
Depth
6in (15cm)

Width (unstretched)
20in (50cm)

TENSION
34 sts & 34 rows = 4in (10cm)
over stitch pattern.

ABBREVIATIONS
See page 11

A nice, quick project, this one – straight
out of the 1940s onto your head! Worked
in a very simple chevron stitch, we've used
a variegated yarn for a more modern take.

DIFFICULTY
++┼┼┼

14

DIRECTIONS

Cast on 170 sts.

Row 1   K.

Row 2   *K2 tog tbl, k5, inc in next 2 sts, k6, k2 tog; rep from * to end.

Row 3   K.

Row 4   As Row 2.

Row 5   P.
Rep Rows 4 & 5 until work measures 4in (10cm) ending with 4th row of patt.

SHAPE TOP

Row 1   *P2 tog, p13, p2 tog tbl; rep from * to end (150 sts).

Row 2   *K2 tog tbl, k4, inc in next 2 sts, k5, k2 tog; rep from * to end (150 sts).

Row 3   *P2 tog, p11, p2 tog tbl; rep from * to end (130 sts).

Row 4   *K2 tog tbl, k3, inc in next 2 sts, k4, k2 tog; rep from * to end.

Row 5   *P2 tog, p9, p2 tog tbl; rep from * to end (110 sts).

Row 6   *K2 tog tbl, k2, inc in next 2 sts, k3, k2 tog; rep from * to end.

Row 7   *P2 tog, p7, p2 tog tbl; rep from * to end (90 sts).

Row 8   *K2 tog tbl, k1, inc in next 2 sts, k2, k2 tog; rep from * to end.

Row 9   *P2 tog, p5, p2 tog tbl; rep from * to end (70 sts).

Row 10   *K2 tog tbl, inc in next 2 sts, k1, k2 tog; rep from * to end.

Row 11   *P2 tog, p3, p2 tog tbl; rep from * to end (50 sts).

Row 12   *K2 tog tbl, k1, k2 tog; rep from * to end (30 sts).

Row 13   P.

Row 14   *Sl 1, k2 tog, psso; rep from * to end.

Row 15   P.

Row 16   *K2 tog; rep from * to end.

MAKING UP

Break off yarn, thread end through remaining sts, draw up and fasten off. Sew side seam. Lay flat, spray with water and allow to dry. Sew a narrow tuck along each line of decreasings at the 'points'. Darn in ends.

CHIGNON CAP

MATERIALS
Anchor Artiste metallic, 80% viscose/
20% polyester, 109yds (100m) per 25g
as follows:

1 x 25g in Shade #342 (Black) (MC)

1 x 25g in Shade #302 (Silver) (CC)

1 pair 3.25mm (US #3) needles

2.25mm (US #B/1) crochet hook

40in (1m) x 1in (2.5cm) wide
grosgrain ribbon

SIZING
Bottom edge
20in (51cm)

Top edge
9¼in (23.5cm)

Height (including brim)
4½in (11.5cm)

TENSION
36 sts & 46 rows = 4in (10cm)
over main stitch.

ABBREVIATIONS
See page 11

This 1950s head-piece is knitted in a simple slip stitch with a garter stitch brim, and adds interest to a plain ponytail or bun. We've knitted it in sparkling metallic yarn to turn it into a glittering evening accessory.

DIFFICULTY
++┼┼┼

DIRECTIONS

CROWN

With CC, cast on 133 sts
(this will form the outer edge).

Rows 1–2 With CC, k.

Row 3 (WS) With MC, *k1, yf, sl 1 purlwise, yb; rep from * to last st, k1.

Row 4 (RS) With MC, *p1, yb, sl 1 knitwise, yf; rep from * to last st, p1.

Row 5 With CC, k to end.

Row 6 (Dec row 1) With CC, k10, *k2 tog, k20; rep from * to last 13 sts, k2 tog, k11 (127 sts). Rep Rows 1–5.

Dec row 2 K9, *k2 tog, k19; rep from * to last 11 sts, k2 tog, k9 (121 sts). Rep Rows 1–5.

Dec row 3 K10, *k2 tog, k18; rep from * to last 11 sts, k2 tog, k9 (115 sts). Rep Rows 1–5.

Dec row 4 K10, *k2 tog, k17; rep from * to last 10 sts, k2 tog, k8 (109 sts). Rep Rows 1–5.

Dec row 5 K9, *k2 tog, k16; rep from * to last 10 sts, k2 tog, k8 (103 sts). Rep Rows 1–5.

Dec row 6 K9, *k2 tog, k15; rep from * to last 9 sts, k2 tog, k8 (97 sts). Rep Rows 1–5.

Dec row 7 K8, *k2 tog, k14; rep from * to last 9 sts, k2 tog, k9 (91 sts). Rep Rows 1–5.

Dec row 8 K8, *k2 tog, k13; rep from * to last 8 sts, k2 tog, k6 (85 sts). Rep Rows 1–5.

Dec row 9 K7, *k2 tog, k8; rep from * to last 8 sts, k2 tog, k6 (77 sts). Rep Rows 1–5.

Dec row 10 K7, *k2 tog, k7; rep from * to last 7 sts, k2 tog, k5 (69 sts). Work 3 more rows in patt.

Next row With MC, cast off.

BRIM

With MC and RS facing, pick up and k around outer edge of crown as follows:

1 st in first st, *kfb, pick up and k next 3 sts; rep from * to end. Work in garter-st until 19 rows have been completed.

Next row K1, *k2 tog, k3; rep from * to end. Cast off. With RS facing, 2.25mm crochet hook and CC, work a row of dc (sc) along short ends of crown, omitting brim. Turn.

Next row Sl st in each dc (sc) across. Break off. Work along opposite edge to correspond. Fold brim in half to WS and sew in place.

MAKING UP

Pin out the cap, spray with water and allow to dry, shaping brim as desired. Close each end of brim at back of hat and sew in place. Cut ribbon in 4 equal parts. Sew 1 piece to each end of brim at back opening and at top of crown. Darn in ends and tie as illustrated.

KNITTED COLLAR

20

MATERIALS
Rico Maxi Cotton, 100% mercerized cotton, 612yds (560m) per 100g, as follows:

1 x 100g in Natural

1 pair 2mm (US #0) needles

2mm (US #B/1) crochet hook

SIZING
Width (shoulder to shoulder)
12in (30.5cm)

Depth (top of back neck–bottom edge)
6½ in (16.5cm)

TENSION
Approx 11 sts & 15 rows = 1in (2.5cm) over main stitch pattern.

ABBREVIATIONS
See page 11

PATTERN & STITCH NOTES
When counting sts and casting off, don't forget to allow for the st lost in each patt in the 1st and 4th rows. The border is created with moss-st.

If you've never tackled lace knitting, this pretty early 1940s collar is an easy project to start you off. It's a versatile accessory that can add an alternative touch to a simple outfit. Don't be put off by its intricate appearance; the stitch is easily created over six rows. If your crochet skills aren't up to scratch, omit the shell edging for a plainer look.

DIFFICULTY
++┼┼┼

22

DIRECTIONS

FRONT
Cast on 48 sts and work
in moss-st as follows:

Row 1   (RS) *K1, p1; rep from * to end.

Row 2   *P1, k1; rep from * to end.
          Rep these 2 rows for ½in (1.5cm).

          Work in patt with moss-st borders
          as follows:

Row 1   Moss-st 6, *k2 tog, yrn, k2 tog;
          rep from * to last 6 sts, moss-st 6.

Row 2   Moss-st 6, *p1, (k1, p1) into yrn, p1;
          rep from * to last 6 sts, moss-st 6.

Row 3   Moss-st 6, k to last 6 sts, moss-st 6.

Row 4   Moss-st 6, p2, *p2 tog, yrn, p2 tog;
          rep from * to last 8 sts, p2, moss-st 6.

Row 5   Moss-st 6, k2, *k1, (k1, p1) into yrn, k1;
          rep from * to last 8 sts, k2, moss-st 6.

Row 6   Moss-st 6, p to last 6 sts, moss-st 6.
          These 6 rows form the patt.

          Cont in patt until work measures 2½in
          (6.5cm) from cast-on edge, ending
          with a Row 2 or 5 of patt.

Next row Cast on 36 sts, moss-st 42, patt 36,
          moss-st 6, cast on 36 sts (120 sts).

Next row Moss-st 42, patt 36, moss-st 42.
          Rep this row until work measures ½in
          (1.5cm) from cast-on edges at sides,
          ending with a Row 2 or 5 of patt.
          Keeping continuity of patt, work in lace
          patt with moss-st borders as follows:

Next row Moss-st 6, patt 108, moss-st 6.
          Rep this row until work measures
          3½in (9cm) from first cast-on edge,
          ending with a Row 2 of patt.

SHAPE NECK

Next row Moss-st 6, patt 49, cast off next 10 sts, patt to last 6 sts, moss-st 6. Now keeping continuity of patt and moss-st border, work on this second set of 55 sts, dec 1 st at neck edge in every row until 38 sts remain. Cont without shaping until work measures 6in (15cm) from first cast-on edge, ending at side edge.

SHAPE SHOULDERS

Next row Cast off 6, patt to end.

Next row Patt to end.
Rep these 2 rows 4 times more.
Cast off. Rejoin yarn at neck edge to rem sts and work to match first side.

BACK

Work as given for Front until work measures 3½in (9cm) from first cast-on edge, then cont in patt with moss-st borders without shaping until work measures 5½in (14cm) from first cast-on edge, ending with a Row 2 of patt.

SHAPE NECK

Next row Moss-st 6, patt 40, cast off next 28 sts, patt to last 6 sts, moss-st 6. Now work on this second set of 46 sts as follows:

Row 1 Cast off 6 sts, work to last 2 sts, work 2 tog.

Row 2 Cast off 3 sts, work to end.
Rep these 2 rows once more.

Row 5 Cast off 6 sts, work to end.

Row 6 Work to end.
Rep last 2 rows twice more. Cast off. Rejoin yarn at neck edge to rem sts and work to end. Now work on these 46 sts to match first side.

NECK BANDS
BACK

Cast on 8 sts and work in moss-st for approx 4in (10cm) or long enough to fit along back neck edge. Cast off.

FRONT

Cast on 8 sts and work in moss-st for approx 6in (15cm) or long enough to fit along front neck edge. Cast off.

MAKING UP

Press pieces lightly on WS using a warm iron over a damp cloth. Sew on neck borders.

SHOULDER BANDS

With 2mm crochet hook, work a border of dc (sc) along back shoulder edges and a similar border along front shoulder edges making 5 ch button loops at equal intervals, last button loop at top of neck band. Sew on buttons. Darn in ends.

SHELL EDGING FOR OUTER EDGES (OPTIONAL)

Worked in multiples of 4 + 1 sts:
Sl 1 in first st. *Sk next st, work 5 htr (hdc) in next st, sk next st, sl st in next st; rep from * to end.

For corners, work as follows: ch1, sl st in first st on next edge, cont working in patt.

HEADSCARF

MATERIALS
Handmaiden Lace Silk, 100% silk,
984yds (900m) per 100g, as follows:

2 x 100g in Pewter

1 pair 5mm (US #8) needles

3mm (US #C/2–D/3) crochet hook

Sequins (optional)

SIZING
Length
50in (125cm)

Width
24in (60cm)

TENSION
18 sts & 28 rows = 4in (10cm)
over stitch pattern.

ABBREVIATIONS
See page 11

This lacy 1940s headscarf will give any outfit
an air of mystery. Knitted here in silk for
a more luxurious finish, it has a voluminous
'fascinator' scarf section shaped using short
rows, and is easily worked by repeating one
row of pattern. We've knitted it with a plain
cap, but you could also finish it with sequins
as the original pattern directed.

DIFFICULTY
+++++

DIRECTIONS

FASCINATOR

Cast on 105 sts and work 1 patt row as follows:

Patt row	(RS) K2, *yrn, k3, sl the first of these 3 sts over the other 2 sts (sl this st from behind); rep from * to the last st, k1. This row forms the patt. Cont in patt, shaping as follows:
Row 1	Work patt row to the last 9 sts, turn.
Row 2	Work patt row to end.
Row 3	Work patt row to the last 18 sts, turn.
Row 4	Work patt row to end.
Row 5	Work patt row to the last 27 sts, turn.
Row 6	Work patt row to end.
Row 7	Work patt row to the last 36 sts, turn.
Row 8	Work patt row to end. Cont in this way, working 9 sts fewer every other row until the 20th row has been completed (working patt row across 15 sts).
Row 21	Patt 6, turn.
Row 22	Patt 6. Now work 12 rows in patt across all sts. Rep these 34 rows (i.e. shaping Rows 1–22, then 12 rows in patt across all sts) 10 times more, then rep Rows 1–22 once more. Cast off fairly loosely, leaving the last loop on the needle.

Now on this same needle with last loop of cast-off edge, pick up and k 128 sts along inner curved edge (129 sts).

CAP

Next row	K2 tog, p2 tog, k2 tog, *p1, k2 tog; rep from * to the last 6 sts, p2 tog, k2 tog, p2 tog (84 sts). Work 6 rows in patt on these 84 sts. Now work in moss-st, shaping as follows:

Row 1	(K1, p1) 4 times, k1, p3 tog, (k1, p1) 9 times, k3 tog, (p1, k1) 9 times, p3 tog, (k1, p1) 9 times, k3 tog, (p1, k1) 4 times, p1.
Row 2	(P1, k1) 4 times, p3 tog, (k1, p1) 8 times, k3 tog, (p1, k1) 8 times, p3 tog, (k1, p1) 8 times, k3 tog, (p1, k1) 4 times.
Row 3	(K1, p1) 3 times, k1, p3 tog, (k1, p1) 7 times, k3 tog, (p1, k1) 7 times, p3 tog, (k1, p1) 7 times, k3 tog, p1, (k1, p1) 3 times (60 sts). Now work 6 rows in patt without shaping.
Next row	Moss-st 6, *work 3 tog, moss-st 12; rep from * to the last 9 sts, work 3 tog, moss-st 6.
Next row	Moss-st 5, *work 3 tog, moss-st 10; rep from * to the last 8 sts, work 3 tog, moss-st 5.
Next row	Moss-st 4, *work 3 tog, moss-st 8; rep from * to the last 7 sts, work 3 tog, moss-st 4 (36 sts). Now work 6 rows in patt without shaping.
Next row	Moss-st 3, *work 3 tog, moss-st 6; rep from * to the last 6 sts, work 3 tog, moss-st 3.
Next row	Moss-st 2, *work 3 tog, moss-st 4; rep from * to the last 5 sts, work 3 tog, moss-st 2 (20 sts).
Next row	*K2 tog; rep from * to end. Break off yarn, thread through rem sts, draw up and fasten off.

MAKING UP

Work a picot edge in crochet all around edge of fascinator (see below). Pin the piece out taking care not to stretch, then spray with water and allow to dry. Sew rows of sequins to the shaped centre part, using the moss-st bands as a guide (optional). Darn in ends.

PICOT EDGING

Make one dc (sc) into first st of scarf edge, *3 ch, dc (sc) into first ch, 3 dc (sc) along scarf edge; rep from * to end.

MAN'S SCARF AND GLOVES IN A FOUR-COLOUR PATTERN

The perfect autumn/winter project, this cosy 1940s scarf and pair of gloves are given extra warmth by the slip stitch pattern and our choice of an alpaca/silk/cashmere blend yarn.

SCARF MATERIALS
Juno Alice Sock Yarn, 70% baby alpaca/ 20% silk/10% cashmere, 437yds (400m) per 100g as follows:

1 x 100g in Velvet (A)

1 x 100g in Golden Peach (B)

1 x 100g in Orangerie (C)

1 x 100g in Savannah (D)

1 pair 3mm (US #2–3) needles

SCARF SIZING
Length	Width
36in (90cm)	7in (17.5cm)

SCARF TENSION
28 sts & 44 rows = 4in (10cm) over main stitch pattern.

SCARF PATTERN & STITCH NOTES
A feature of the main st is a version of a sl st and requires a certain amount of daring! You will need to take the st off the needle and let it drop by 2 rows, then pick up that same st (2 rows down), plus the 2 slack loops formed by dropping the st. This is referred to as 'let the next st down 2 rows'. Have courage; once you've done it a couple of times it's easier than it sounds.

GLOVES MATERIALS
As per Scarf materials and quantities.

You will also need:
Small amount of contrasting yarn

1 set of 4 x 2mm (US #0) dpns

GLOVES SIZING
All around hand
8in (20cm)

Length of palm
5in (12.5cm)

GLOVES TENSION
38 sts & 52 rows = 4in (10cm) over main stitch pattern.

ABBREVIATIONS
See page 11

DIFFICULTY
+++++

SCARF DIRECTIONS

With 3mm needles and A, cast on 96 sts.

Row 1	P.
Row 2	K.
Row 3	P. Now work in patt as follows: Change to B.
Row 1	*K3, let next st down 2 rows, then k that st and the 2 loops formed tog; rep from * to the last 4 sts, k4.
Row 2	P. Change to C.
Row 3	*K1, let next st down 2 rows, then k that st and the 2 loops formed tog, k2; rep from * to end.
Row 4	P. Change to D and rep Rows 1 & 2. Change to A and rep Rows 3 & 4. These 8 rows form the patt. Cont in patt until work measures 36in (90cm), ending with patt Row 8. Cont with A.
Next row	K.
Next row	P. Cast off.

MAKING UP
Pin the piece out, then spray with water and allow to dry. Fold lengthwise and join one end and side edges on the WS. Turn scarf to RS, join open end neatly and press.

FRINGE
Cut a strip of cardboard 2¼in (5.5cm) wide and wind C around it. Cut yarn along one edge of cardboard and using 4 lengths of yarn at a time, make a fringe at each end of scarf as follows: fold lengths of yarn in half and draw loop through edge of knitting with a crochet hook. Knot by drawing ends through loop. Rep evenly along ends of scarf.

GLOVES DIRECTIONS

LEFT GLOVE
With 2mm dpns and A, cast on 60 sts and work in rnds of k2, p2 rib until work measures 2½in (6.5cm).

Next rnd	*K6, k twice in the next st; rep from * to the last 4 sts, k4 (68 sts). Distribute sts so that you have 24 sts on two needles and 20 on the last. K 3 rnds. Now work in patt as follows: Change to B.
Rnd 1	*K3, let next st down 2 rows, then k that st and the 2 loops formed tog; rep from * to end.
Rnd 2	K. Change to C.
Rnd 3	*K1, let next st down 2 rows, then k that st and the 2 loops formed tog, k2; rep from * to end.
Rnd 4	K. Change to D and rep Rnds 1 & 2. Change to A and rep Rnds 3 & 4. These 8 rnds form the patt. Cont in patt until work measures 5½in (14cm) from cast-on, ending with either Rnd 2 or 4. Keeping the continuity of the patt, work as follows:
Next rnd	Patt 22 sts, break off yarn, now k next 12 sts with an odd length of yarn in a different colour, rejoin previous yarn and work in patt to end.
Next rnd	K.
Next rnd	Patt 22, k12, patt to end. Now cont in patt across all sts until work measures 7¼in (18cm) from cast-on. Keeping continuity of patt, work as follows:
Next rnd	Patt 8, sl these 8 sts onto a st-holder, cast on 2 sts, k these 2 sts, work in patt to the last 8 sts, cast on 2 sts, sl last 8 sts onto st-holder.

Cont in patt but omitting dropped sts in the 4 cast-on sts until work measures 7½in (19cm) from cast-on. Break off B, C and D.

THIRD FINGER

Next rnd With A, k10, cast on 4 sts, sl next 36 sts onto a piece of yarn, k10. Place these 24 sts evenly onto 3 needles and k in rnds with A until finger measures 2¾in (7cm) or required length.

Next rnd *K2 tog, k1; rep from * to end.

Next rnd K.

Next rnd *K2 tog; rep from * to end. Break off yarn and thread through rem sts. Draw up tightly and fasten off on WS.

MIDDLE FINGER

With A, pick up and k 4 sts from cast-on edge of third finger. Now k the first 8 sts from rem 36 sts, cast on 4 sts and k the last 8 sts from piece of yarn. Place these 24 sts evenly on 3 needles and k in rnds until finger measures 3¼in (8cm) or required length. Shape top and fasten off as given for Third Finger.

FIRST FINGER

With A, pick up and k 4 sts from cast-on edge of middle finger, then k rem 20 sts. Place these 24 sts evenly on 3 needles and k in rnds until finger measures 2¾in (7cm) or required length. Shape top and fasten off as for Third Finger.

FOURTH FINGER

With A pick up and k 4 sts from cast-on edge at base of Third Finger. Now k 8 sts from st-holder at back of glove, sl rem 8 sts from st-holder onto another needle and k in rnds on these 20 sts until finger measures 2½in (6.5cm) or required length.

Next rnd *K2 tog, k1; rep from * to last 2 sts, k2.

Next rnd K.

Next rnd *K2 tog, rep from * to end. Fasten off as for Third Finger.

THUMB

Unpick the odd piece of yarn knitted over 12 sts, halfway up palm of glove and sl the 24 loops on 3 needles. With A, k in rnds until Thumb measures 2¼in (5.5cm) or required length. Shape top and fasten off as for Third Finger.

RIGHT GLOVE

Work exactly as given for Left Glove until work measures 5½in (14cm) from lower edge, ending with either Rnd 2 or 4.

Next rnd Patt 34 sts, break off yarn, now k next 12 sts with an odd length of yarn in a different colour. Rejoin previous yarn and work in patt to end.

Next rnd K.

Next rnd Patt 34, k12, patt to end. Now complete as given for Left Glove.

TWELVE POLO MODE HATS

This cheeky collection of 1950s hats is a superb example of how versatile knitted fabric can be: take varying lengths of rectangular ribbed knitting and turn them into twelve stylish pieces of headgear. The patterns are about as simple as you'll ever get, plus you get to have fun making up the trimmings. Pom-pom makers at the ready…

DIFFICULTY
+++++

MATERIALS

The hats use the following yarns:

Rowan Pure Wool DK, 100% wool, 137yds (125m) per 50g

Rowan Pure Wool 4-ply, 100% wool, 174yds (160m) per 50g

Orkney Angora 4-ply, 100% angora, 218yds (200m) per 25g

DMC Petra Cotton (Size 3), 100% cotton, 306yds (280m) per 100g

HAT NO.1
2 x 50g Rowan Pure Wool DK
in Shade #010 (Indigo)
1 pair 3.75mm (US #5) needles
1 pair 4.5mm (US #7) needles
3mm (US #C/2–D/3) crochet hook

HAT NO.2
1 x 50g Rowan Pure Wool 4-ply
in Shade #450 (Eau-De-Nil)
1 pair 3mm (US #2–3) needles
1 pair 3.75mm (US #5) needles

HAT NO.3
2 x 50g Rowan Pure Wool DK
in Shade #010 (Indigo)
1 pair 3.75mm (US #5) needles
1 pair 4.5mm (US #7) needles

HAT NO.4
2 x 50g Rowan Pure Wool DK
in Shade #007 (Cypress)
1 pair 3.75mm (US #5) needles
1 pair 4.5mm (US #7) needles
3mm (US #C/2–D/3) crochet hook

HAT NO.5
1 x 50g Rowan Pure Wool 4-ply
in Shade #451 (Porcelaine) (A)
1 x 25g Orkney Angora 4-ply
in Shade #26 (Natural) (B)
1 pair 3mm (US #2–3) needles
1 pair 3.75mm (US #5) needles

HAT NO.6

1 x 25g Orkney Angora
in Shade #009 (Azure)
Small amount of gold crochet
or embroidery thread
1 pair 3mm (US #2–3) needles
1 pair 3.75mm (US #5) needles

HAT NO.7

2 x 50g Rowan Pure Wool 4-ply
in Shade #410 (Indigo) (A)
1 x 50g Rowan Pure Wool 4-ply
in Shade #451 (Porcelaine) (B)
1 x 50g Rowan Pure Wool 4-ply
in Shade #450 (Eau-De-Nil) (C)
1 pair 3mm (US #2–3) needles
1 pair 3.75mm (US #5) needles

HAT NO.8

1 x 50g Rowan Pure Wool DK
in Shade #010 (Indigo) (A)
1 x 50g Rowan Pure Wool DK
in Shade #007 (Cypress) (B)
1 pair 3.75mm (US #5) needles
1 pair 4.5mm (US #7) needles

HAT NO.9

2 x 50g Rowan Pure Wool 4-ply
in Shade #410 (Indigo)
1 pair 3mm (US #2–3) needles
1 pair 3.75mm (US #5) needles

HAT NO.10

2 x 50g Rowan Pure Wool 4-ply
in Shade #450 (Eau-De-Nil)
1 pair 3mm (US #2–3) needles
1 pair 3.75mm (US #5) needles
3mm (US #C/2–D/3) crochet hook

HAT NO.11

1 x 50g Rowan Pure Wool 4-ply
in Shade #410 (Indigo) (A)
1 x 25g DMC Petra Cotton 3
in Shade #5145 (Light Blue) (B)
1 pair 3mm (US #2–3) needles
1 pair 3.75mm (US #5) needles
3mm (US #C/2–D/3) crochet hook

HAT NO.12

2 x 50g Rowan Pure Wool DK
in Shade #007 (Cypress)
1 pair 3.75mm (US #5) needles
1 pair 4.5mm (US #7) needles
3mm (US #C/2–D/3) crochet hook

SIZING

To fit one average-size head
(the rib stitch gives a broad flexibility).
See individual patterns for length.

TENSION

Per 4in (10cm), measured over
unstretched k1, p1 rib:

4-ply/Angora
3mm needles: 48 sts & 38 rows
3.75mm needles: 46 sts & 37 rows
4.5mm needles: n/a

DK
3.75mm needles: 39 sts & 32 rows
4.5mm needles: 34 sts & 28 rows

ABBREVIATIONS

See page 11

PATTERN & STITCH NOTES

All hats are worked in a simple
k1, p1 rib st.

Where the hat has a rolled-up brim
and/or cap, the 'Making Up' directions
will instruct you to 'secure'. This is best
carried out by sewing the roll with a
couple of catch sts at a few separate
points around the hat — if you sew all
the way around, this will tighten the
otherwise elastic nature of the rib.

Please also note that when sewing
a seam on a hat that has a rolled-up
brim and/or cap, the seam for the
rolled-over sections should be worked
on the RS of the hat so that the outer
seam will be invisible.

HAT NO.1

HAT NO.2

36

HAT NO.3

HAT NO.4

HAT NO.5

HAT NO.6

DIRECTIONS

HAT NO.1
Length
12in (30cm)

With 3.75mm needles, cast on 100 sts. Work 1¼in (3cm) in k1, p1 rib, then change to 4.5mm needles and cont in rib until work measures 6¾in (17cm). Change to 3.75mm needles and cont in rib until work measures 12in (30cm). Cast off ribwise.

MAKING UP

Do not press. Join side edges of strip to form a round. Roll over cast-off edge at top and secure, then roll up lower edge and secure. Using 9 strands of yarn, crochet a chain 15in (37.5cm) in length and finish each end with a 2in (5cm) tassel. Tie the chain around the hat just below the roll. Darn in all ends.

HAT NO.2
Length
7in (17.5cm)

With 3mm needles, cast on 120 sts. Work 1¼in (3cm) in k1, p1 rib, then change to 3.75mm needles and cont in rib until work measures 6¼in (15.5cm). Change to 3mm needles and cont in rib until work measures 7in (17.5cm). Cast off ribwise.

MAKING UP

Do not press. Join side edges of strip to form a round. Roll up lower edge and secure; gather top edge and finish with a long tassel. Darn in all ends.

HAT NO.3
Length
7in (17.5cm)

With 3.75mm needles, cast on 100 sts. Work 1¼in (3cm) in k1, p1 rib, then change to 4.5mm needles and cont in rib until work measures 6¾in (17cm). Change to 3.75mm needles and cont in rib until work measures 7in (17.5cm). Cast off.

MAKING UP

Do not press. Join side edges of strip to form a round. Fold work with seam at side edge, and catch-stitch cast-off (top edge) tog at centre. Now fold the 2 outer edges towards centre and stitch these to the centre mark. Darn in all ends.

HAT NO.4
Length
12in (30cm)

With 3.75mm needles, cast on 100 sts. Work 1¼in (3cm) in k1, p1 rib, then change to 4.5mm needles and cont in rib until work measures 6¾in (17cm). Change to 3.75mm and cont in rib until work measures 12in (30cm). Cast off ribwise.

MAKING UP

Do not press. Join side edges of strip to form a round. Gather cast-off edge, draw up and fasten off. Crochet a chain 3½in (9cm) in length. Sew one end to gathered section and trim opposite end with a large pom-pom. Darn in all ends.

HAT NO.5
Length
7in (17.5cm)

With 3mm needles and A, cast on 120 sts. Work 1¼in (3cm) in k1, p1 rib, then change to 3.75mm needles and B. *Work 2 rows in rib, change yarn to A and work 2 rows in rib; rep from * until work measures 6¼in (15.5cm). Change to 3mm needles and cont in ribbed stripe sequence until work measures 7in (17.5cm). Cast off ribwise.

MAKING UP

Do not press. Join side edges of strip to form a round. Gather cast-off edge, draw up and fasten off, then trim with a pom-pom made with both A and B. Darn in all ends.

HAT NO.6
Length
7in (17.5cm)

With 3mm needles, cast on 120 sts. Work 1¼in (3cm) in k1, p1 rib, then change to 3.75mm needles and cont in rib until work measures 6¼in (15.5cm). Change to 3mm needles and cont in rib until work measures 7in (17.5cm). Cast off ribwise.

MAKING UP

Do not press. Join side edges of strip to form a round. Run a gathering thread 1½in (4cm) below the cast-off edge; draw up and fasten off. Using gold thread double, crochet a chain 15in (38cm) in length, and finish each end with a gold tassel. Tie chain around hat over gathering thread. Darn in all ends.

HAT NO.7
Length
7in (17.5cm)

With 3mm needles and A, cast on 120 sts. Work 1¼in (3cm) in k1, p1 rib, then change to 3.75mm needles and cont in rib in the following stripe sequence: 4 rows B, 8 rows C, 6 rows A, 6 rows B, 2 rows C, 4 rows A, 2 rows B, 4 rows C, 2 rows A, 4 rows B, 6 rows C. Change to 3mm needles and A. Cont in rib until work measures 7in (17.5cm). Cast off ribwise.

MAKING UP
Do not press. Join side edges of strip to form a round. Fold work with seam at side edge, and catch-stitch cast-off (top edge) tog at centre, then catch-stitch each 'fold' tog. Finish outer edge of each 'fold' with a small pom-pom of the yarns used. Darn in all ends.

HAT NO.8
Length
12in (30cm)

With 3.75mm needles and A, cast on 100 sts. Work 1¼in (3cm) in k1, p1 rib, then change to 4.5mm needles and cont in rib until work measures 3¾in (9.5cm). Change to B and cont in rib until work measures 8in (20cm). Change to 3.75mm needles and rib 3 rows, then change to A and cont in rib until work measures 12in (30cm). Cast off ribwise.

MAKING UP
Do not press. Join side edges of strip to form a round. Roll down top and secure, then roll up lower edge over a thin pad of cotton wool and secure. Darn in all ends.

HAT NO.9
Length
14in (35cm)

With 3mm needles, cast on 120 sts. Work 1¼in (3cm) in k1, p1 rib, then change to 3.75mm needles and cont in rib until work measures 6¼in (15.5cm). Change to 3mm needles, cont in rib until work measures 14in (35cm). Cast off ribwise.

MAKING UP
Do not press. Join side edges of strip to form a round. Roll down top and secure, then roll up lower edge and secure. Darn in all ends.

HAT NO.10
Length
14in (35cm)

With 3mm needles, cast on 120 sts. Work 1¼in (3cm) in k1, p1 rib, then change to 3.75mm needles and cont in rib until work measures 6¼in (15.5cm). Change to 3mm needles and cont in rib until work measures 14in (35cm). Cast off ribwise.

MAKING UP
Do not press. Join side edges of strip to form a round. Sew cast-off edges tog and finish with a row of fringe. Crochet a chain 13in (32.5cm) in length and tie around centre of hat. Roll up lower edge and secure. Darn in all ends.

HAT NO.11
Length
14in (35cm)

With 3mm needles and A, cast on 120 sts. Work 1¼in (3cm) in k1, p1 rib, then change to 3.75mm needles and cont in rib until work measures 1½in (4cm). *Change to B and work 4 rows in rib. Change to A and work 4 rows in rib; rep from * until work measures 6¼in (15.5cm). Change to 3mm needles and cont in striped rib sequence until work measures 14in (35cm). Cast off ribwise.

MAKING UP
Do not press. Join side edges of strip to form a round. Gather cast-off edge, draw up and fasten off. With B, crochet a chain 3in (7.5cm) in length and attach it to the hat, then create a tassel and attach it to the chain. Darn in all ends.

HAT NO.12
Length
12in (30cm)

With 3.75mm needles, cast on 100 sts. Work 1¼in (3cm) in k1, p1 rib, then change to 4.5mm needles and cont in rib until work measures 6¾in (17cm). Change to 3.75mm and cont in rib until work measures 12in (30cm). Cast off ribwise.

MAKING UP
Do not press. Join side edges of strip to form a round. Crochet a chain 2in (5cm) in length and attach it to the hat. Create a large pom-pom and attach it to the chain. Fold up lower part of hat to form a tuck (see picture) and secure. Darn in ends.

38

HAT NO.7

HAT NO.8

HAT NO.9

HAT NO.10

HAT NO.11

HAT NO.12

TRIM ANKLE SOCKS

We're used to knitting our socks on double-pointed needles in the round, but vintage sock patterns are often knitted on two needles with seams at the sides of the foot and back of the leg. Have no fear of seams in socks; this 1940s pair are incredibly comfortable, and perfect for anyone who hasn't made the dpns leap into the world of socks.

MATERIALS
Regia 4-ply, 75% new wool/25% polyamide, 229yds (210m) per 50g, as follows:

1 x 50g Shade #2018 (Ice Blue) (MC)

1 x 50g in Shade #324 (Marine) (CC)

1 pair 3mm (US #2–3) needles

SIZING
Leg length
(from cuff to beg of heel shaping)
3 1/2in (9cm) / 3 1/2in (9cm)

Leg circumference
(actual size, will stretch)
6 1/2in (16.5cm) / 7 1/2in (19cm)

Foot length (from heel to toe)
8 1/2in (21.5cm) / 9 1/2in (24cm)

TENSION
Approx 40 sts & 58 rows = 4in (10cm) over stitch pattern.

ABBREVIATIONS
See page 11

PATTERN & STITCH NOTES
Work with 1 ball of each shade, carrying spare colour up side of work. Always take yarn very loosely across the back of the slipped sts.

The stitch pattern is fairly tightly woven; it does stretch but can produce a tight-fitting sock. If in doubt about sizing, knit the instructions for the larger size and adjust length accordingly.

When you have divided the sock for Heel and Foot, the pattern directs you to cont in pattern for 5 [6]in (12.5 [15]cm) or desired length: in order to establish your desired foot length, measure the sole of your own foot and subtract 2in (5cm) (the length of the toe).

The heel is shaped using short rows — we have kept to the original pattern instructions, which use an alternative method to w&t to eliminate holes. This method does provide a more 'decorative' effect (i.e. the turn is visible), so you may prefer to use your own w&t methods.

DIFFICULTY
++┼┼┼

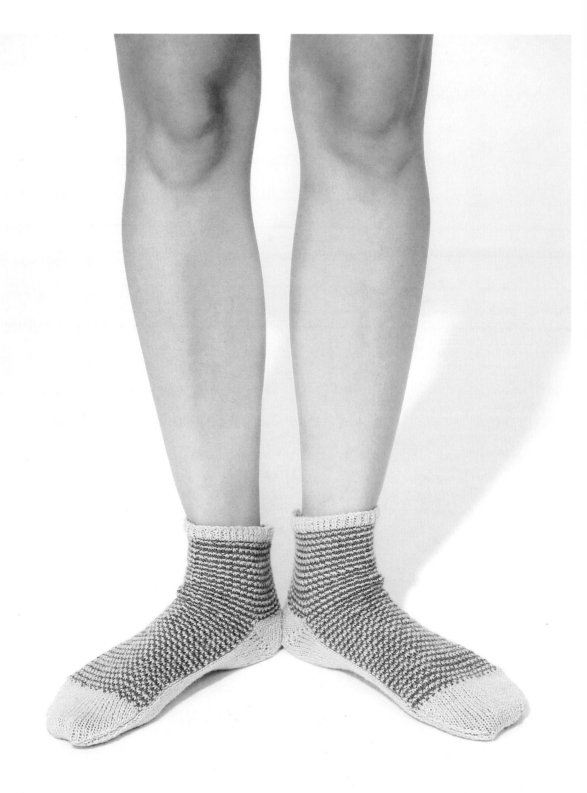

DIRECTIONS

With MC, cast on 64 [72] sts.
Work ½in (1.5cm) in k1, p1 rib.
Cont in patt as follows:

Row 1 (RS) With B, *k1, sl 1; rep from * to end.

Row 2 With B, *k1, yf, sl 1, yb; rep from * to end.

Row 3 With A, rep Row 1.

Row 4 With A, rep Row 2.
These 4 rows form the patt.
Cont in patt until work measures
3½in (9cm), ending with a WS row.

DIVIDE FOR HEEL AND FOOT
Next row (RS) Patt 49 [56], turn.

Next row Patt 34 [40], turn.
Cont in patt on these 34 [40] sts for
instep for 5 [6]in (12.5 [15]cm) or desired
length (see Pattern & Stitch Notes),
ending with a WS row.

SHAPE TOE
Cont with MC, break off CC.

Row 1 K to end.

Row 2 P1 [4], (p3, p2 tog, p3) 4 times, p1 [4]
(30 [36] sts).

Row 3 K1, sl 1, k1, psso, k to last 3 sts, k2 tog,
k1 (28 [34] sts).

Row 4 P.
Rep last 2 rows until 10 [12] sts rem.
Leave sts on st-holder.

SHAPE HEEL
Return to rem 30 [32] sts for the heel
and sl onto one needle with side
edges to centre forming back seam.

With RS of work facing and MC, work
2 rows St-st, then cont as follows:

Row 1 K to last st, turn.

Row 2 P to last st, turn.

Row 3 K to last st of previous row, turn.

Row 4 P to last st of previous row, turn.
Rep last 2 rows 9 times.

Next row K across sts of previous row, pick up
thread between st just worked and
next st and k tog with next st to avoid
a hole, turn.

Next row P across sts of previous row, pick up
thread between st just worked and
next st and p tog with next st to avoid
a hole, turn.
Rep last 2 rows until all sts are on
one needle, ending with a WS (p) row
(30 [32] sts).

Cont in St-st until work measures
the same as the top part of foot
to beg of toe shaping, ending with
a WS (p) row.

Work 2 more rows in St-st, then rep
Rows 3 & 4 for previous 'Shape Toe'
section until 10 [12] sts rem. Now place
two sets of sts tog and graft neatly
(see page 8).

MAKING UP
Sew foot and leg seams. Darn in ends.
Press lightly on WS using a warm iron
over a damp cloth.

BOOK BAG

44

This great 1940s crochet bag is tougher than it looks. Working two strands of the flexible metallic polyester and strong Shetland wool together gives it a combined strength and a great industrial look. Neat of appearance, the Tardis-like bag has a middle section so you can organize your life, storing your tablet in one pocket and your knitting in another!

MATERIALS
Anchor Artiste Metallic, 80% viscose/
20% polyester, 109yds (100m)
per 25g as follows:

2 x 25g in Shade #301

Shetland Supreme Jumper Weight
(Undyed), 100% Shetland wool,
188yds (172m) per 50g as follows:

2 x 50g in Shade #2003 (Shaela)

4mm (US #G/6) crochet hook

Two buckles

SIZING
The finished bag is approx 14in (35cm)
wide and 10in (25cm) long. The flap is
approx 5in (12.5cm).

TENSION
4 sts & 5 rows = 1in (2.5cm)
over stitch pattern.

ABBREVIATIONS
See page 11

PATTERN NOTES
The pattern is written in UK crochet
terms with the US equivalent in brackets.

DIFFICULTY
++++++

DIRECTIONS

FRONT
Make 54 ch, turn.

Row 1 Work 1 dc (sc) in 2nd ch from hook tand in each st of ch. Ch 1, turn. 53 dc (sc).

Row 2 Work 1 dc (sc) in each dc (sc) of previous row. Ch 1, turn.

Row 3 Sl st in each dc (sc) of previous row. Ch 1, turn. Rep Rows 2 & 3 for approx 10in (25cm), or desired length.

CENTRE SECTION
Work exactly the same as Front.

BACK AND FLAP
Work same as Front, but make the piece about 15in (37.5cm) long.

GUSSETS
Make 2 — one to sew between Front and Centre section and another between Centre and Back.

Make a ch long enough to go around 2 sides and lower edge of Front. Then ch 25 additional sts to allow for working up.

Row 1 Work 1 dc (sc) in 3rd ch from hook, and in each st of ch until work measures same as one side of Front. Then to shape for corner, *insert hook in next ch, draw loop through, insert hook in next st, draw loop through, insert hook in next st, draw loop through. Yarn around hook and draw through all loops on hook (2 sts decreased)*. Work dc (sc) into next set of sts, which will form the bottom of the bag, rep from * to * (making 2 more decs for corner), then work same number of dc (sc) as were made for other side.

Row 2 Work a sl st in each st, ch 1, turn.

Rows 3–8 Make a dc (sc) in previous dc (sc) for odd rows, work 2 sts decreased at corners over decs of previous row. Work sl sts for all even rows.

Rows 9–16 Work dc (sc) in previous dc (sc) on odd rows (increasing 2 sts at corners where decs were made previously). Work sl sts for all even rows. Make another piece the same.

HANDLE
Make 70 ch, turn.

Rows 1–18 Work in same st patt as Front.

STRAPS (MAKE 4 ALIKE)
Make 12 ch, turn.

Rows 1–4 Work in same st patt as Front.

MAKING UP
Block carefully to correct dimensions. Sew the gussets to the Front and Centre pieces, then to the Back using a firm stitch. Sew handle piece across top of flap, leaving loop for handle as illustrated. Darn in ends. Sew two straps to the flap, and two straps to the main part of the bag. Attach buckles.

ATTRACTIVE JUMPER WITH SLANTING YOKE IN CABLE STITCH

This late 1940s/early 1950s design is literally given a great twist with the slanting cable-stitch yoke. Worked in rib to give elasticity (which in turn ensures a close fit), the pattern is straightforward to follow.

DIFFICULTY
++┼┼┼

MATERIALS
Koigu Premium Merino, 100% merino wool, 175yds (160m) per 50g, as follows:
7 x 50g in Shade #1043

1 pair 3.25mm (US #3) needles

1 pair 2.75mm (US #2) needles

Cable needle or spare dpn

5 buttons

SIZING
TO FIT BUST SIZES
34in / 36in / 38in / 40in
(85cm / 90cm / 95cm / 100cm)

ACTUAL FINISHED MEASUREMENTS
(OVER UNSTRETCHED RIB)
Bust
15in / 16in / 17in / 18in
(37.5cm / 40cm / 42.5cm / 45cm)

Length (shoulder–underarm)
6in / 6¼in / 6½in / 6¾in
(15cm / 15.5cm / 16.5cm / 17cm)

Length (hem–underarm)
14½ in / 14¾in / 15in / 15¼in
(36.5cm / 37cm / 37.5cm / 38cm)

Armhole depth
6in / 6¼in / 6½in / 6¾in
(15cm / 15.5cm / 16.5cm / 17cm)

Shoulder to shoulder
11in / 12in / 12¾in / 13½in
(27.5cm / 30cm / 32cm / 34cm)

Inner sleeve
4in / 4in / 4in / 4in
(10cm / 10cm / 10cm / 10cm)

TENSION
44 sts & 40 rows = 4in (10cm) using 3.25mm needles over unstretched rib.

ABBREVIATIONS
See page 11

PATTERN & STITCH NOTES
The jumper is mostly knitted in k2, p2 rib. The cable stitch is carried out as follows: to 'cable 6', sl next 4 sts onto a dpn and leave at front of work, k next 2 sts, sl the 2 p sts from spare needle back onto left-hand needle and p them, then k the 2 sts from spare needle.

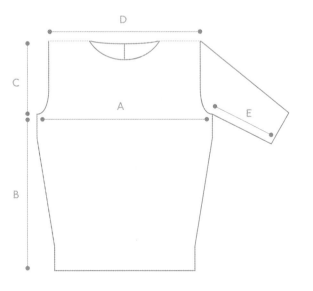

FRONT
With 2.75mm needles, cast on 114 [122, 134, 142] sts.

Rib row 1   Rib (RS): P2, (k2, p2) to end.

Rib row 2   Rib: K2 (p2, k2) to end.
Rep 1st and 2nd rib rows until Front measures 2in (5cm).

Change to 3.25mm needles, cont in rib but inc 1 st at each end of next row and every following 4th row until there are 164 [174, 184, 194] sts, gradually working the extra sts into the rib.

Cont without shaping until Front measures 12¼ [11½, 12, 13]in (30.5 [29, 30, 32.5]cm).
Now commence cables as follows:

Cable row 1   K1 [2, 1, 2], p2, (cable 6, as explained in 'pattern notes' on page 48) 2 [1, 2, 3] times, rib to end.

Rib 11 rows.

Cable row 2   K1 [2, 1, 2], p2, (cable 6, p2) 5 [3, 5, 6] times, rib to end.

SIZES 36 & 38 ONLY
Rib 11 rows.
Extra cable row: k- [2, 1, -], p- [2, 2, -], (cable 6, p2) - [6, 8, -] times.

ALL SIZES
Rib 9 rows.

SHAPE ARMHOLE
Next 2 rows   Cast off 5 sts, rib to end (154 [164, 174, 184] sts).

Next row   P2 tog, p0 [1, 0, 1], k2, p2, (cable 6, p2)
(Cable row 3)   7 [8, 10, 8] times, rib to last 2 sts, p2 tog (152 [162, 172, 182] sts).

Rib 11 rows, AT THE SAME TIME dec 1 st at each end of every row (130 [140, 150, 160] sts).

Cable row 4   P2 tog, p0 [1, 0, 1], (cable 6, p2) 9 [10, 12, 10] times, rib to last 2 sts, dec 1 (128 [138, 148, 158] sts).

A   15 (16, 17, 18)in
37.5 (40, 42.5, 45)cm

B   14½ (14¾, 15, 15¼)in
36.5 (37, 37.5, 38)cm

C   6 (6¼, 6½, 6¾)in
15 (15.5, 16.5, 17)cm

D   11 (12, 12¾, 13½)in
27.5 (30, 32, 34)cm

E   4 (4, 4, 4)in
10 (10, 10, 10)cm

Rib 3 rows , AT THE SAME TIME dec I st at each end of every row (122 [132, 142, 152] sts). Rib 8 rows.

Cable row 5   K0 [1, 0, 1], p2 [2, 1, 2], k2, p2, (cable 6, p2) 10 [12, 14, 12] times, rib to end. Rib 11 rows.

Cable row 6   K0 [1, 0, 1], p2 [2, 1, 2], k2, p2, (cable 6, p2) 14 [15, 17, 15] times, rib to end.

SIZE 40 ONLY
Rib 11 rows.

Cable row 7   K1, p2, k2, p2, (cable 6, p2) 18 times, k1.

ALL SIZES
Rib 5 rows.

SHAPE NECK

Next row   Rib 50 [54, 56, 60]; turn. Leaving rem 72 [78, 86, 92] sts on a spare needle, cont only on first set of sts as follows:

Rib 5 rows, AT THE SAME TIME dec I st at neck edge on each of these rows (45 [49, 51, 55] sts).

SIZES 34 & 38 ONLY

Next row (Cable row)   P2 [-, 1, -], k2, p2, (cable 6, p2) 4 [-, 5, -] times, then sl next 4 sts onto cable needle and leave at front of work, k next 2 sts, sl the 2 p sts from spare needle back onto left-hand needle and p them, then k2 tog from spare needle (44 [-, 50, -] sts).

SIZES 36 & 40 ONLY

Next row (Cable row)   K- [1, -, 1], p2, k2, p2, (cable 6, p2) 5 times, (cable 6) - [0, -, 1] times, dec I (- [48, -, 54] sts).

ALL SIZES
Rib 11 rows, ending on a WS row, AT THE SAME TIME dec I st at neck edge on the first 8 of these rows (36 [40, 42, 46] sts).

SHAPE SHOULDERS

Row 1   (RS) Cast off 9 [10, 10, 11] sts, rib to end.

Row 2   Rib.

Rows 3–4   Rep last 2 rows once.

Row 5   Cast off 9 [10, 11, 12] sts, rib to end. Rib I row, then cast off rem 9 [10, 11, 12] sts.

Return to 72 [78, 86, 92] sts on spare needle, and with RS facing, slip first 22 [24, 30, 32] sts onto a st-holder for neck, rejoin yarn and rib rem 50 [54, 56, 60] sts. Cont on these sts as follows:

Rib 5 rows dec I st at neck edge on every row (45 [49, 51, 55] sts).

SIZES 34 & 38 ONLY

Next row (Cable row)   Sl next 4 sts onto a double-pointed needle and leave at front of work, k2 tog from left-hand needle, sl the 2 p sts from spare needle back onto left-hand needle and p them, then k the 2 sts from spare needle. Then p2, (cable 6, p2) 4 [-, 5, -] times, rib to end.

SIZES 36 & 40 ONLY

Next row (Cable row)   K2 tog, p- [2, -, 0], k- [0, -, 2], p- [0, -, 2], (cable 6, p2) - [5, -, 6] times, rib to end.

ALL SIZES
Rib 10 rows, ending on a RS row, AT THE SAME TIME dec I st at neck edge on the first 8 of these rows (36 [40, 42, 46] sts).

Now shape shoulder as first side, decreasing at the armhole edge.

BACK
With 2.75mm needles, cast on 114 [122, 134, 142] sts and work the first and 2nd rib rows of Front until piece measures 2in (5cm). Change to 3.25mm needles and cont in rib, AT THE SAME TIME inc I st at each end of next row and every following 4th row until there are 164 [174, 184, 194] sts, gradually working the extra sts into the rib. Cont without shaping until Back measures 14½ [14¾, 15, 15¼]in (36.5 [37, 37.5, 38]cm), or length matches Front to armholes.

SHAPE ARMHOLES
Cast off 5 sts at beginning of next 2 rows (154 [164, 174, 184] sts), then dec I st at each end of following 16 rows (122 [132, 142, 152] sts). Cont without shaping until work measures 1¾ [2, 2¼, 2½]in (4.5 [5, 5.5, 6]cm) from beginning of armhole shaping, ending on a WS row.

BACK OPENING

Now divide for back opening as follows:

Next row	(RS) Rib 64 [68, 74, 77]; turn. Leaving rem 58 [64, 68, 75] sts on a spare needle, cont on first set of sts as follows:
Next row	Rib to end.

*Rib 8 more rows. Make a buttonhole on next 2 rows as follows:

Next row	Rib to last 5 sts, cast off 2, rib 3.
Next row	Rib 3, cast on 2, rib to end.*

Rep from * to * 3 times more.
Work should measure same as Front from beginning of armhole shaping to beginning of shoulder shaping.

SHAPE SHOULDERS

Row 1	(RS) Cast off 9 [10, 10, 11] sts, rib to end.
Row 2	Rib to end.
Rows 3–4	Rep last 2 rows once.
Row 5	Cast off 9 [10, 11, 12] sts, rib to end.
Row 6	Rep Row 2.
Row 7	Rep Row 5.

Leave rem 28 [28, 32, 31] sts on a st-holder for neck band. With RS of Back facing you, join yarn to inner end of the 58 [64, 68, 75] sts on spare needle, and proceed for second side as follows:

Cast on 6 sts to form an underwrap, then rib to end of row (64 [70, 74, 81] sts). Cont in rib to match the first side (without buttonholes), then shape shoulders by working shaping at armhole edge as first side. Leave rem 28 [30, 32, 35] sts on a st-holder for neck band.

SLEEVES (MAKE 2)

With 2.75mm needles, cast on 86 [86, 90, 90] sts and work in k2, p2 rib as follows:

Row 1	(RS) P2 (k2, p2); rep to end.
Row 2	K2 (p2, k2); rep to end.

Cont until work measures 1¼in (3cm). Change to 3.25mm needles, cont in rib, AT THE SAME TIME inc 1 st at each end of next row and every following 3rd row until there are 106 [106, 112, 112] sts. Cont without shaping until work measures 4in (10cm) from cast-on edge, ending on a WS row.

SHAPE SLEEVE CAP

Cast off 5 sts at start of next 2 rows (96 [96, 102, 102] sts), then dec 1 st at beginning of every row until 60 [60, 64, 64] sts rem, then dec 1 st at each end of following 12 rows (36 [36, 40, 40] sts).

Next row	K2 tog to end of row. Cast off rem 18 [18, 20, 20] sts.

NECK BAND

Join shoulder seams, taking care to retain elasticity of the rib by ensuring the seam isn't too tight. With RS of work facing you, join yarn to centre back end of sts on st-holder at left side of Back. Using a 2.75mm needle, work in k2, p2 across these 28 [30, 32, 35] sts, then pick up and k 28 [27, 27, 27] sts along side-front neck edge, rib across the 22 [24, 30, 32] sts on st-holder at front neck, then pick up and k 28 [27, 27, 27] sts along other side of front neck, after which rib across the 28 [28, 32, 31] sts on st-holder, at right side of Back (134 [136, 148, 152] sts).

Rib 3 rows, then make a buttonhole on next 2 rows as follows:

Next row	Rib to last 5 sts, cast off 2, rib 3.
Next row	Rib 3, cast on 2, rib to end. Rib another 5 rows, then cast off ribwise.

MAKING UP

Do not block or press pieces as this will flatten the rib and detract from the elasticity of the stitch. Sew side and sleeve seams. Sew sleeves into armholes. Sew down base of the Back neckline underwrap on WS. Sew on buttons. Darn in ends.

BLOUSE FRONT

Blouse fronts were an economical and popular
solution during the yarn-rationed war years.
A knitted or crochet sleeveless front with
a net or fabric backing was worn under
a jacket or cardigan to create the illusion
of a complete garment. This delicate crochet
1940s example is a backless halterneck,
but you could add a back, if liked.

MATERIALS
BC Garn Jaipur Fino, 100% mulberry
silk, 328yds (300m) per 50g, as follows:

2 [2] x 50g in Shade #H58 (Mauve)

3mm (US #2–D/3) crochet hook

1 button

SIZING
TO FIT SIZES
34–36in / 38–40in
(85cm–90cm / 95–100cm)

ACTUAL FINISHED MEASUREMENTS
Width
18in / 21in (45cm / 52.5cm)

Length (shoulder–hem)
18in / 21in (45cm / 52.5cm)

TENSION
1 pattern repeat = 1⅕in (3cm) square.

ABBREVIATIONS
See page 11

PATTERN & STITCH NOTES
10 ch makes up 1 pattern. The blouse
front is a simple square in shape.

The pattern is written in UK crochet
terms with the US equivalent in brackets.

DIFFICULTY
++┼┼┼

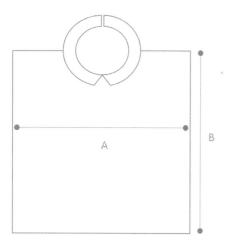

A 18 (21)in
   45 (52.5)cm

B 18 (21)in
   45 (52.5)cm

DIRECTIONS

FRONT
Make 152 [172] ch.

Row 1   Miss 1 ch, 1 dc (sc) into each ch,
              1 ch, turn.

Row 2   1 dc (sc) into first dc (sc), 1 dc (sc) into
              next dc (sc), *5 ch, miss 3 dc (sc), 1 dtr
              (trc) into next dc (sc), 5 ch, miss 3 dc
              (sc), 1 dc (sc) into each of next 3 dc (sc);
              rep from * ending row with 2 dc (sc)
              instead of 3 dc (sc).

Row 3   8 ch, *1 dc (sc) into 5th ch next to dtr
              (trc), 1 dc (sc) into dtr (trc), 1 dc (sc) into
              next ch, 4 ch, 1 dtr (trc) into 2nd dc (sc),
              4 ch; rep from * omitting the
              4 ch at end of row.

Row 4   9 ch, *1 dc (sc) into each of 3 dc (sc),
              5 ch, 1 dtr (trc) into dtr (trc), 5 ch; rep
              from * ending row with 1 dtr (trc) into
              4th of the 8 ch and omitting last 5 ch.

Row 5   1 ch, *1 dc (sc) into dtr (trc), 1 dc (sc) into
              next ch, 4 ch, 1 dtr (trc) into 2nd dc (sc),
              4 ch, 1 dc (sc) into 5th ch; rep from *,
              ending row with 2 dc (sc) into ch.

Row 6   1 ch, *1 dc (sc) into each of 2 dc (sc),
              5 ch, 1 dtr (trc) into dtr (trc), 5 ch, 1 dc
              (sc) into next dc (sc); rep from * ending
              row with 1 dc (sc) into last dc (sc).

              Rep from Row 3 to Row 6 until work
              measures 15 [18]in (37.5 [45]cm), ending
              with a 3rd patt row.

SHAPE NECK
Next row 19 ch, *1 dc (sc) into each of 3 dc (sc),
              5 ch, 1 dtr (trc) into dtr (trc), 5 ch; rep
              from * 4 [5] times more, 1 dc (sc) into
              each of 3 dc (sc), 5 ch, 1 dtr (trc) into
              dtr (trc), 1 dtr (trc) into next dc (sc), turn
              and work on this piece only for one
              side of neck.

Next row 1 ch, 1 dc (sc) into 2nd dtr (trc), 1 dc (sc)
              into next ch, work in patt to end of row.

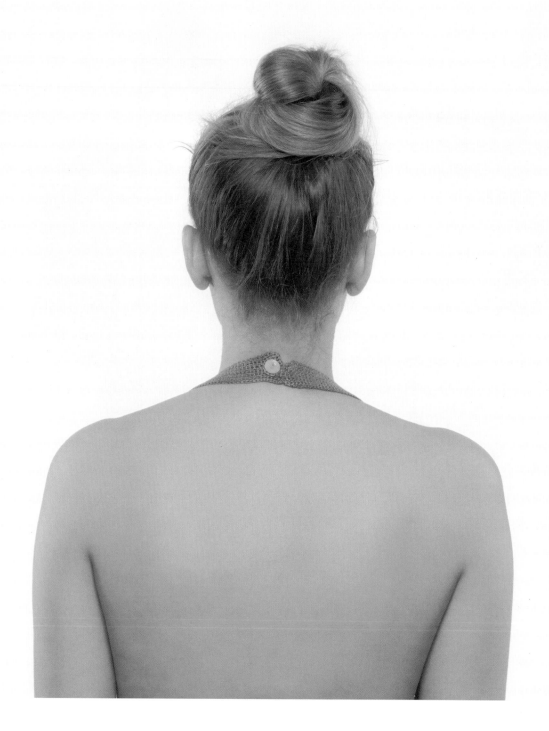

Work 4 more rows decreasing in the same manner as these 2 rows (1½ patts will be decreased), then cont without shaping on 5 [6] patts in width until work measures 18 [19]in (45 [47.5]cm), ending with a 3rd or 5th patt row. Break off. Rejoin yarn so that 2 patts are left in centre, rejoining yarn into 3rd of 3 dc (sc).

Next row   5 ch, 1 dtr (trc) into dtr (trc), work in patt to end.

Next row   Work in patt ending row with 1 dc (sc) into last dtr (trc).

Work 4 more rows decreasing in the same manner as last 2 rows (1½ patts will be decreased), then complete to match other side.

COLLAR
Begin in centre front of neck and work 40 dc (sc) evenly around right half of neck up to shoulder, make 30 ch, turn.

Row 1   Miss 2 ch, 1 dc (sc) into each ch, 1 dc (sc) into each dc (sc), 2 ch, turn.

Row 2   *2 dc (sc) into dc (sc), 1 dc (sc) into each of next 3 dc (sc); rep from * to end, 2 ch, turn.

Row 3   1 dc (sc) into each dc (sc), 2 ch, turn.

Rows 4–5   As Row 3.

Row 6   *2 dc into dc (sc), 1 dc (sc) into each of next 9 dc (sc); rep from * ending with 5 dc (sc), 2 ch, turn.
Work 7 more rows as Row 3. Break off. Make 28 ch, then work 40 dc (sc) evenly around other half of neck beginning at shoulder.

Work to match first side of collar, reversing the shaping rows, as follows:

Row 2   *1 dc (sc) into each of 3 dc (sc), 2 dc (sc) into next dc; rep from * to end.

MAKING UP
Pin the piece out to the correct dimensions, then spray with water and allow to dry. Do not press. The original pattern instructions give you the option to starch the piece, but it's not advisable when using silk yarn.

Sew a button to one side of collar and make a loop on the other side by inserting the crochet hook into the top of the neckband fabric from front to back, draw yarn through and make enough chains to go around the button securely. Insert hook through fabric and sl st to work. Darn in ends.

BLOUSE WITH A ROUND YOKE

A pretty, delicate 1950s jumper knitted in a drop-stitch with picot-edged sleeves and eyelet yoke. The cap sleeves are knitted integrally and the Front and Back are the same, meaning you have to knit only three pieces in all. The high ribbed welt sits at the natural waistline, while the lace stitch gives the jumper some stretch and fit flexibility.

MATERIALS

Wendy Merino 4-ply, 100% wool, 191yds (175m) per 50g, as follows:

5 [6, 6, 6] x 50g in Shade #2376 (Silver)

1 pair 3.25mm (US #3) needles

1 pair 2.75mm (US #2) needles

3.5mm (US #E/4) crochet hook

4 buttons

SIZING

TO FIT SIZES
34in / 36in / 38in / 40in
(85cm / 90cm / 95cm / 100cm)

ACTUAL FINISHED MEASUREMENTS
Bust
33in / 35in / 37in / 39in
(82.5cm / 88cm / 93cm / 98cm)

Length (shoulder–hem)
19in / 19in / 19¾in / 20½in
(47.5cm / 47.5cm / 49.5cm / 51.5cm)

Length (waist–underarm)
12in / 12in / 12¾in / 13½in
(30cm / 30cm / 32cm / 34cm)

Armhole depth
7in / 7in / 7in / 7in
(17.5cm / 17.5cm / 17.5cm / 17.5cm)

Shoulder to shoulder
15½in / 15¾in / 16in / 16¼in
(39cm / 39.5cm / 40cm / 41cm)

Inner sleeve
3in / 3in / 3in / 3in
(7.5cm / 7.5cm / 7.5cm / 7.5cm)

TENSION

8 sts = 1in (2.5cm) & 8 rows = 1½in (3.75cm) using 3.25mm needles over stitch pattern.

ABBREVIATIONS

See page 11

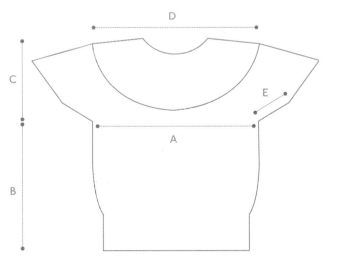

A   16½ (17½, 18½, 19½)in
41 (44, 46.5, 49)cm

B   12 (12, 12¾, 13½)in
30 (30, 32, 34)cm

C   7 (7, 7, 7)in
17.5 (17.5, 17.5, 17.5)cm

D   15½ (15¾, 16, 16¼)in
39 (39.5, 40, 41)cm

E   3 (3, 3, 3) in
7.5 (7.5, 7.5, 7.5)cm

PATTERN & STITCH NOTES

The blouse is mainly knitted in the following st patt (in multiples of 5):

Row 1   (RS) *K4 tog, (k1, p1, k1, p1) into next st; rep from * to end of row.

Row 2   P.

Row 3   K, winding yarn 3 times round needle for every st.

Row 4   P, allowing each group of sts to slide into 1 long loop.

Row 5   *(K1, p1, k1, p1) all into first st, k4 tog; rep from * to end of row.

Row 6   P.

Row 7   Rep Row 3.

Row 8   Rep Row 4.
These 8 rows form the patt.

DIRECTIONS

BACK

With 2.75mm needles, cast on 100 [100, 104, 108] sts. Work in k1, p1 rib for 4in (10cm).

Next row   (WS) *Work 4 [3, 3, 3] sts in rib, work twice into next st; rep from * to end (120 [125, 130, 135] sts).
Change to 3.25mm needles.

Work in main st patt and inc 1 st at each end of 5th row and of every following 4th row until 132 [139, 148, 157] sts are on needle. Cont without shaping until Back measures 12 [12, 12¾, 13½]in (30 [30, 32, 34]cm) ending on a 4th or 8th row of patt.

SHAPE ARMS

Cast on 10 sts at beginning of next 2 rows, then inc 1 st at each end of 3rd row and of every following 4th row until 156 [163, 172, 181] sts are on needle, ending on a 1st or 5th row of patt.

Next row   (WS) P53, cast off 50 [57, 66, 75] sts, p53.

65

SHAPE NECK & SLEEVE

Leave sts for first shoulder on st-holder. Working in patt, cast off 5 sts at beginning of 2nd row and of every following 4th row (i.e. at neck edge), AT THE SAME TIME cont to inc 1 st every 4th row on the sleeve edge as before.

Cont shaping neck and sleeve edge until 32 sts rem (5 cast-off groups have been worked at neck edge). No further neck shaping is worked at this end of the needle, but cont to inc 1 st at beginning of every 4th row for sleeve shaping until 34 sts rem.

Cast off 5 sts at beginning of next row, which commences at sleeve edge, and at beginning of every other row until 9 sts rem. Cast off. With 3.25mm needles, return to the sts left on the st-holder and join yarn at neck edge.

Working in patt, cast off 5 sts at beginning of the 3rd row and of every following 4th row, while cont sleeve shapings AT THE SAME TIME as before.

Cont shaping neck and sleeve edge until 32 sts rem (5 cast-off groups have been worked at neck edge). No further neck shaping is worked at this end of the needle, but cont to inc 1 st at beginning of every 4th row for sleeve shaping until 34 sts rem.

Cast off 5 sts at beginning of the next row, which commences at sleeve edge, and of every other row until 9 sts rem. Cast off.

FRONT

Work exactly as for Back.

SLEEVE BANDS

Join shoulder seams. With 3.25mm needles and RS facing, pick up 78 sts along sleeve edge.

Commencing with a p row, work 7 rows in St-st.

Next row   K2, *yf, k2 tog; rep from * to end. Commencing with a p row, work 7 rows more in St-st. Cast off loosely. Work the second sleeve edge to match.

ROUND YOKE

With 3.25mm needles, cast on 280 [294, 308, 322] sts. Commencing with a k row, work 8 rows in St-st.

Row 9   K2, *yf, k2 tog; rep from * to end. Commencing with a p row, work 7 rows in St-st.

Row 17   *K5, k2 tog; rep from * to end (240 [252, 264, 276] sts).

Row 18   P.

Row 19   Rep Row 9.

Row 20   P.
Commencing with a k row, work 6 rows in St-st.

Row 27   *K4, k2 tog; rep from * to end (200 [210, 220, 230] sts).

Row 28   P.

Row 29   Rep Row 9.

Row 30   P.
Commencing with a k row, work 6 rows in St-st.

Row 37   *K3, k2 tog; rep from * to end (160 [168, 176, 184] sts).

Row 38   P.

Row 39   Rep Row 9.

Row 40   P.
Commencing with a k row, work 6 rows in St-st.

Row 47   *K2, k2 tog; rep from * to end (120 [126, 132, 138] sts).

Row 48   P.

Row 49   Rep Row 9.

Row 50   P.

Row 51   K.

Row 52 P.
Change to 2.75mm needles and
work in k1, p1 rib for 1in (2.5cm).
Cast off ribwise.

MAKING UP
NOTE The crochet edging is written
in UK crochet terms with the US
equivalent in brackets.

Press pieces lightly on WS using
a warm iron over a damp cloth, taking
care to avoid the ribbed welts.
Join yoke by sewing from lower edge
to 3rd row of holes, then turn up
picot-edged hem at outer edge onto
WS. Sew neck edges of Back and Front
behind the picot hem, so that hem
overhangs the lacy fabric and join
of yoke is across one shoulder.

Sew side seams. Turn up hem on WS
of each sleeve edge. Work 4 rows
of dc (sc) along back shoulder, work
one row of dc (sc) along front edge
of shoulder commencing at shoulder
edge, 1 ch, turn.

Next row 1 dc (sc) in 1st dc (sc), *3 ch, miss 2 dc
(sc), 1 dc (sc) in each of next 3 dc (sc),
rep from * 3 times more.
Fasten off.

Sew on buttons to correspond with
buttonholes. Darn in ends.

MAN'S LUMBERJACKET

This excellent gent's lumberjacket was
a very popular style in the late 1940s and
early 1950s. Worn slightly larger than the
usual close-fitting ladies' garments, you get
a great 'boyfriend' cardigan look, the pleated
pockets and garter-stitch collar giving it
some stand-out detail.

MATERIALS

Cascade 220 Superwash Sport,
100% superwash merino wool,
136yds (125m) per 50g, as follows:

7 x 50g in Shade #801 (Army Green)

1 pair 5mm (US #8) needles

18in (45cm) open-ended zip

SIZING

TO FIT BUST SIZES
34–36in / 36–38in / 38–40in
(85–90cm / 90–95cm / 95–100cm)

ACTUAL FINISHED MEASUREMENTS
Bust
37in / 39in / 41in
(93cm / 98cm / 102cm)

Length (shoulder–hem)
22½in / 24in / 25½in
(56.5cm / 60cm / 64cm)

Length (hem–underarm)
13in / 14in / 15in
(32.5cm / 35cm / 37.5cm)

Armhole depth
9½in / 10in / 10½in
(24cm / 25cm / 26.5cm)

Shoulder to shoulder
13¾in / 14in / 15in
(33cm / 35cm / 37.5cm)

Inner sleeve
21in / 21½in / 22in
(52.5cm / 54cm / 55cm)

TENSION

20 sts & 26 rows = 4in (10cm)
over Stocking stitch.

ABBREVIATIONS

See page 11

DIFFICULTY
++┼┼┼

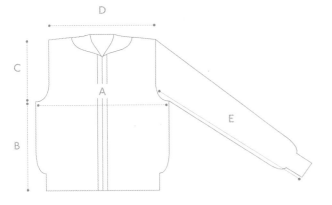

DIRECTIONS

BACK
Cast on 88 [90, 92] sts.
Work in k1, p1 rib for 3in (7.5cm).

Next row (RS) K18 [10, 10], *inc 1, k16 [9, 7], rep from * 3 [7, 9] times to last 19 [10, 10] sts, inc 1, k18 [9, 9] (92 [98, 102] sts).

Next row P.
Cont in St-st until work measures 13 [14, 15]in (32.5 [35, 37.5]cm) from cast-on edge, or required length to armholes, ending on a WS row.

SHAPE ARMHOLES
Cast off 5 sts at beginning of next 2 rows. Then dec 1 st at each end of next and every other row until 66 [70, 74] sts rem.

Cont without shaping until the armhole measures 9½ [10, 10½]in (24 [25, 26.5]cm) from beginning of armhole shaping.

SHAPE SHOULDERS
Cast off 11 [12, 12] sts at beginning of next 4 rows. Cast off rem 22 [22, 26] sts.

LEFT FRONT
Cast on 46 [48, 50] sts.

Row 1 (RS): P1, *k1, p1; rep from * to last 5 sts, k5.

Row 2 K5, rib to end of row.
Rep these 2 rows for 3in (7.5cm), ending on a WS row.

Next row K5 [6, 7], *inc 1, k5; rep from * 5 times, inc 1, k10 [11, 12] (52 [54, 56] sts).

Row 2 K5, p to end of row.
Cont in St-st, remembering to k5 at beginning of every WS (p) row for garter-st border.

SHAPE ARMHOLE
With RS facing, cast off 5 sts, k to end of row. Then dec 1 st at armhole edge until 42 [44, 46] sts rem. Cont without shaping until armhole measures

A 18½ (19½, 20½)in
   46 (49, 51)cm

B 13 (14, 15)in
   32.5 (35, 37.5)cm

C 9½ (10, 10½)in
   24 (25, 26.5)cm

D 13¼ (14, 14½)in
   33 (35, 37.5)cm

E 21 (21½, 22)in
   52.5 (54, 55)cm

4½ [5, 5½]in (11.5 [12.5, 14]cm) from beginning of armhole shaping. Slip the k5 border sts onto a st-holder.

SHAPE NECK

At neck edge dec 1 st on next and every following alt row until 22 [24, 24] sts rem.
Cont without shaping until armhole measures 9½ [10, 10½]in (24 [25, 26.5]cm) from beginning of armhole shaping.

SHAPE SHOULDER

Cast off 11 [12, 12] sts from armhole edge on next and every following alt row.

COLLAR

With RS facing, sl k5 border sts onto knitting needle. Cont in garter-st as follows:

Next row	K1, inc 1, k to last 2 sts, inc 1, k1. Rep last row until 19 sts are on needle, then inc at outer edge only as follows:
Next row	K1, inc 1, k to end.
Next row	K. Rep last 2 rows until 26 sts are on needle. Cont without shaping until collar measures along front neck to centre of back neck. Cast off.

RIGHT FRONT

Cast on 46 [48, 50] sts.

Row 1	(RS): K5, p1, *k1, p1; rep from * to end of row.
Row 2	Rib to last 5 sts, k5. Rep these 2 rows for 3in (7.5cm), ending on a WS row.
Next row	K10 [11, 12], *inc 1, k5; rep from * 5 times, inc 1, k5 [6, 7] (52 [54, 56] sts).
Next row	P to last 5 sts, k5. Finish to match Left Front, working shapings at opposite edges and cont to k5 at the end of every WS (p) row for garter-st border. Work another collar, reversing shapings from previous collar instructions.

SLEEVES (MAKE 2)

Cast on 40 [44, 48] sts. Work in k1, p1 rib for 3in (7.5cm).

Next row	(RS) K2 [4, 6], *inc 1, k3, rep from * to last 2 [4, 6] sts, inc 1, k to end of row (50 [54, 58] sts). Cont in St-st, inc 1 st at each end of every 4th row until 92 [98, 102] sts. Work without shaping until Sleeve measures 21 [21½, 22]in (52.5 [54, 55]cm), or desired sleeve length.

SHAPE SLEEVE CAP

Cast off 6 [4, 5] sts at beginning of next 2 rows (78 [90, 92] sts). Dec 1 st at each end of every following 3rd [2nd, 2nd] row until 62 [64, 66] sts rem, then dec 1 st at each end of every row until 34 [36, 38] sts rem. Cast off.

POCKETS (MAKE 2)

Cast on 48 sts. Cont in St-st without shaping for 5½ [5¾, 6]in (14 [14.5, 15]cm), ending on a WS row.

PLEAT

Next row	K15, cast off 18 sts, k15.
Next row	Work in k1, p1 rib across rem 30 sts. Cont in k1, p1 rib until pocket border measures 1½in (4cm). Cast off.

MAKING UP

Press pieces lightly on WS using a warm iron over a damp cloth. Sew shoulder and side seams. Sew cast-off edges of collar together and sew collar to neck, making sure the collar seam matches the centre of Back. Sew sleeves in armholes. Sew zip to fronts. Fold under pocket pleats and stitch to secure. Attach pockets to each front as illustrated. Darn in ends.

JUMPER IN STRIPES OF TWO COLOURS AND TWO THICKNESSES OF WOOL

This early 1940s jumper looks surprisingly modern: the two thicknesses of yarn along with the method of knitting the bodice from side to side give it interesting texture, while the cowl neck is an elegant detail. We've finished it with matching knitted buttons, but you could use contrasting ones. This is quick to knit on larger needles than usual.

DIFFICULTY
+++++

MATERIALS

Excelana DK, 100% wool, 130yds (119m) per 50g ball, as follows:

6 [6, 7, 7] x 50g in Persian Grey (MC)

Excelana 4-ply, 100% wool, 174yds (159m) per 50g ball, as follows:
3 [3, 3, 4] x 50g in Nile Green (CC)

1 pair 5.5mm (US #9) needles

1 pair 3mm (US #2–3) needles (for buttons — optional)

5 x 1in (2.5cm) button covers (or 6 buttons)

Strong clip for the cowl neck (optional)

SIZING

TO FIT SIZES
34in / 36in / 38in / 40in
(85cm / 90cm / 95cm / 100cm)

ACTUAL FINISHED MEASUREMENTS
(OVER UNSTRETCHED RIB)
Bust
25in / 25in / 31in / 31in
(62.5cm / 62.5cm / 77.5cm / 77.5cm)

Length (shoulder–hem)
21in / 22¼in / 23in / 24½in
(52.5cm / 55.5cm / 58cm / 61.5cm)

Length (waist–underarm)
16in / 17in / 17½in / 18in
(40cm / 42.5cm / 44cm / 45cm)

Armhole depth
5in / 5¼in / 5½in / 6½in
(12.5cm / 13cm / 14cm / 16.5cm)

Shoulder to shoulder
15½in / 15½in / 17in / 17in
(39cm / 39cm / 42.5cm / 42.5cm)

Inner sleeve
18in / 18in / 19in / 19in
(45cm / 45cm / 47.5cm / 47.5cm)

TENSION

17 sts & 34 rows = 4in (10cm) using 5.5mm needles over unstretched ribbed pattern.

ABBREVIATIONS

See page 11

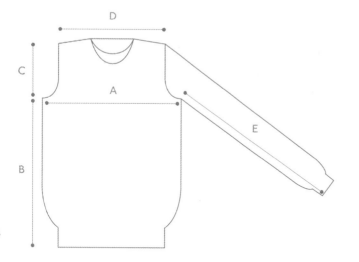

PATTERN & STITCH NOTES

Please note that cast-off edges are usually tighter than cast-on edges — as the bodice is knitted from side to side, take extra care not to cast off too tightly.

The raised stripes are worked by creating 6 rows of reverse Stocking stitch ridges with the dark DK (MC), and 2 rows of right-side Stocking stitch in the lighter 4-ply (CC).

Where a MC stripe is worked for the Front and Back, the pattern will instruct you to 'work MC stripe' — follow the instructions for Rows 9–14 of the Front. Where a CC stripe is worked, the pattern will instruct you to 'work CC stripe' — follow the instructions for Rows 15–16 of the Front.

DIRECTIONS

FRONT
With 5.5mm needles and MC, cast on 40 [44, 46, 48] sts.

Row 1	(RS) P.
Row 2	Cast on 4 sts, k to end (44 [48, 50, 52] sts).
Row 3	P.
Row 4	Cast on 4 sts, k to end (48 [52, 54, 56] sts).
Row 5	P.
Row 6	Cast on 4 sts, k to end (52 [56, 58, 60] sts).
Row 7	Change to CC, k to end.
Row 8	Cast on 4 sts, p to end (56 [60, 62, 64] sts).
Row 9	Change to MC, k to end.
Row 10	K.
Row 11	P.
Row 12	K.

A 12½ (12½, 15½, 15½)in
   31.5 (31.5, 39, 39)cm

B 16 (17, 17½, 18)in
   40 (42.5, 44, 45)cm

C 5 (5¼, 5½, 6½)in
   12.5 (13, 14, 16.5)cm

D 15½ (15½, 17, 17)in
   39 (39, 42.5, 42.5)cm

E 18 (18, 19, 19)in
   45 (45, 47.5, 47.5)cm

Row 13	P.	Cowl row 4	K.
Row 14	K.	Cowl row 5	P44, w&t.
Row 15	Change to CC, k to end.	Cowl row 6	K.
Row 16	P.	Cowl row 7	Change to CC, k34, w&t.

SHAPE ARMHOLE

Next row — Change to MC, cast on 3 [4, 4, 5] sts, k to end (59 [64, 66, 69] sts).

Cowl row 8 — P.

Cowl row 9 — Change to MC, k32, w&t.

Next row — K.

Cowl row 10 — K.

Next row — Cast on 3 [4, 4, 5] sts, p to end (62 [68, 70, 74] sts).

Cowl row 11 — P30, w&t.

Cowl row 12 — K.

Next row — K.

Cowl row 13 — P28, w&t.

Cast on 14 [14, 16, 18] sts (for edge of armhole) and p to end (76 [82, 86, 92] sts).

Cowl row 14 — K.

Cowl row 15 — Change to CC, k26, w&t.

SHAPE SHOULDER

Next row — K.

Cowl row 16 — P.

Next rows — Work CC stripe (i.e. rep Rows 15–16).

Cowl row 17 — Change to MC, work along all the sts on the needle, creating k sts where the previous row was a k row, and p sts where the previous row was a p, to blend in with centre MC stripe. Remember to incorporate wrapped sts.

Next rows — Work MC stripe (i.e. rep Rows 9–14).

Next row — *Change to CC, cast on 2 sts and k to end (78 [84, 88, 94] sts).

Next row — P.*
Work MC stripe.
Rep from * to * (80 [86, 90, 96] sts).
Work MC stripe.
Rep from * to * (82 [88, 92, 98] sts).

Cowl rows 18–22 — Cont to work MC stripe (i.e. 1 row k, 1 row p, 1 row k, 1 row p, 1 row k).

The second half of the cowl is worked in reverse, as follows:

SIZES 38 & 40 ONLY
Work MC stripe.
Rep from * to * (- [-, 94, 100] sts).

Cowl rows 23–24 — Rep Cowl Rows 15–16.

Cowl row 25 — Change to MC, k28, w&t.

ALL SIZES
Work MC stripe, then work CC stripe.**

Cowl row 26 — K.

Cowl rows 27–28 — Rep Cowl Rows 11–12.

COWL NECK
The following rows form the cowl neck.

Cowl row 29 — P32, w&t.

Cowl row 1 — Change to MC, k64, w&t.

Cowl row 30 — K.

Cowl row 2 — K.

Cowl rows 31–32 — Rep Cowl Rows 7–8.

Cowl row 3 — P54, w&t.

Cowl row 33 — Change to MC, k44, w&t.

Cowl row 34	K.
Cowl rows 35–36	Rep Rows 3–4.
Cowl row 37	P64, w&t.
Cowl row 38	K.
	Cont to work rem half of the bodice, again reversing the shapings of the first half as follows:
Next row	Change to CC, k to end of row, working along all sts on the needle and remembering to incorporate the wrapped sts.
Next row	P.
	SHAPE SHOULDER Work MC stripe.
Next row	*Change to CC, cast off 2 sts, k to end (80 [86, 92, 98] sts).
Next row	P.* Work MC stripe. Rep from * to * (78 [84, 90, 96] sts). Work MC stripe. Rep from * to * (76 [82, 88, 94] sts). SIZES 38 & 40 ONLY Work MC stripe Rep from * to * (- [-, 86, 92] sts). ALL SIZES Work MC stripe, then work CC stripe.
Next row	Change to MC, k to end.
Next row	K.
	SHAPE ARMHOLE
Next row	Cast off 14 [14, 16, 18] sts, p to end (62 [68, 70, 74] sts).
Next row	K.
Next row	Cast off 3 [4, 4, 5] sts, p to end (59 [64, 66, 69] sts).
Next row	K.
Next row	Change to CC, cast off 3 [4, 4, 5] sts, k to end (56 [60, 62, 64] sts).

Next row	P. Work MC stripe.
Next row	Change to CC, k to end.
Next row	Cast off 4 sts, p to end (52 [56, 58, 60] sts).
Next row	Change to MC, k to end.
Next row	Cast off 4 sts, k to end (48 [52, 54, 56] sts).
Next row	P.
Next row	Cast off 4 sts, k to end (44 [48, 50, 52] sts).
Next row	P.
Next row	Cast off 4 sts, k to end (40 [44, 46, 48] sts). Cast off 40 [44, 46, 48] sts loosely enough to resemble cast-on tension.
	BACK Work as for Front up to **. Then work in stripes without the cowl neck shaping until there are 5 MC stripes across the Back, as follows:
Neck rows 1–6	Work MC stripe.
Neck rows 7–8	Work CC stripe. Rep these last 8 rows 4 times more (making 5 MC stripes), ending after a CC stripe. Now work as for Front from 'Shape Shoulder' to end. Cast off rem 40 [44, 46, 48] sts loosely enough to resemble cast-on tension.
	SLEEVES (MAKE 2) With 5.5mm needles and MC, cast on 44 [46, 48, 50] sts, work in k2, p2 rib until cuff measures 2½in (6.5cm).
Row 1	(RS) With MC, p3 [4, 5, 6], *p twice into next st, p1; rep from * to last 3 [4, 5, 6] sts, p twice into next st, p2 [3, 4, 5] (64 [66, 68, 70] sts).
Row 2	K.
Row 3	P.

Row 4 K.

Row 5 P.

Row 6 K.

Row 7 Change to CC, k to end.

Row 8 P.

Rep Rows 1–8 until sleeve measures
18 [18, 19, 19]in (45 [45, 47.5, 47.5]cm)
or desired length from cast-on edge
when stretched slightly, ending with an
8th row. Work Rows 1–4 once more.

SLEEVE CAP SHAPING
Still keeping to the stripe patt, cast
off 5 sts at beginning of next 2 rows.
(54 [56, 58, 60] sts).

Dec 1 st at each end of every other row
until 24 [26, 28, 30] sts rem.

Work 0 [0, 2, 4] rows without shaping.

Dec 1 st at each end of next 4 [5, 5, 6]
rows (16 [16, 18, 18] sts). Cast off
quite tightly.

WAIST RIBBING (MAKE 2)
With 5.5mm needles and MC, cast on
84 [84, 92, 92] sts. Work in k2, p2 rib
until work measures 3in (7.5cm). Cast
off loosely.

MAKING UP
Do not block or press pieces as this
will flatten the rib and detract from
the elasticity of the stitch.

Sew the shoulder and side seams. Sew
the sleeve seams. Sew in the sleeves.
Join the Waistband pieces into a ring.
Mark the centre front and centre back
of the lower edge of the jumper and
mark the centres of the two lengths of
ribbing. Attach the Waistband to the
lower edge of the jumper by pinning
seams to seams and centres to centres,
then stretch the band between these
points until it fits, accommodating any
ease on either side. Oversew carefully
so that the stitching will stretch with
the fabric. Darn in ends.

BUTTONS (OPTIONAL)
With 3mm needles and A, cast on 8 sts.
Cont as follows:

Row 1 K.

Row 2 P.

Row 3 K.

Row 4 Change to B, k to end.

Row 5 P.

Row 6 Change to A, k to end.

Rows 7–9 Rep Rows 1–3.

Rows 10–16 Rep Rows 4–9.
Cast off. Sew a running stitch around
the edge of the button and draw up
slightly. Place the button cover into
the centre and pull the gathering stitch
tightly. Make 4 more. Attach buttons
evenly to centre of Front.

TO ARRANGE THE COWL
Turn the top edge down inside the
jumper until the two shortest thin
stripes are folded in half. Sew securely
in position, running this turning off to
nothing at the shoulder. Gather the
centre front down in pleats to suit
the wearer, sew firmly and then stitch
the clip over the thickest part of the
fold, and sew the buttons down the
centre stripe. The edge of the back
neck must be firmly oversewn and
the thread pulled up until the neck
fits snugly at the back.

LADY'S JUMPER WITH
A DOUBLE SCARF COLLAR

We've given this elegant, close-fitting lacy 1930s jumper a nautical touch using navy and white contrasting yarn. Our version maintains its original short torso length, but you can easily add a little length to the main body before the armhole shaping.

MATERIALS
Drops Baby Merino, 100% merino wool, 191yds (175m) per 50g ball, as follows:

9 [10, 10, 10] x 50g in Shade #13 (Navy Blue) (MC)

1 [1, 1, 1] x Shade #01 (White) (CC)

1 pair 3.75mm (US #5) needles

1 pair 2.75mm (US #2) needles

3 small buttons for the back opening

SIZING
TO FIT BUST SIZES
34in / 36in / 38in / 40in
(85cm / 90cm / 95cm / 100cm)

ACTUAL FINISHED MEASUREMENTS
Bust
34in / 36in / 38in / 40in
(85cm / 90cm / 95cm / 100cm)

Length (shoulder–hem)
18in / 18½in / 19in / 19½in
(45cm / 46.5cm / 48cm / 49cm)

Length (hem–underarm)
11½in / 12in / 12in / 12¼in
(29cm / 30cm / 30cm / 31cm)

Armhole depth
6½in / 6½in / 7in / 7¼in
(16.5cm / 16.5cm / 17.5cm / 18cm)

Shoulder to shoulder
13in / 13½in / 14in / 14½in
(32.5cm / 34cm / 35cm / 36.5cm)

Inner sleeve
17½in / 18in / 18in / 18¼in
(44cm / 45cm / 45cm / 46cm)

TENSION
28 sts & 40 rows = 4in (10cm) using 3.75mm needles over stitch pattern.

ABBREVIATIONS
See page 11

PATTERN & STITCH NOTES
The main stitch pattern is worked over 10 sts and 16 rows. The scarves are worked in moss-st.

DIFFICULTY
+++++

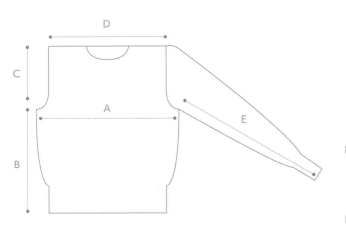

DIRECTIONS

BACK

With 2.75mm needles and MC, commence at the lower edge by casting on 106 [114, 118, 124] sts and work 4in (10cm) in k1, p1 rib. Change to 3.75mm needles.

Next row (RS) K9 [7, 6, 5], *k twice into the next st, k7 [8, 6, 5], rep from * to last 9 [8, 7, 5] sts, k twice into the next st, k to end (118 [126, 134, 144] sts).

Next row P.

Patt row 1 (RS) Sl 1, k3 [2, 1, 1], *k2 tog, k3, pick up the underlying thread between the st on the working needle and the next st to be worked, (k1, p1) into the picked-up thread (increasing 2 sts and forming a hole), k3, sl 1, k1, psso; rep from * to last 4 [3, 2, 2] sts, k4 [3, 2, 2].

Patt row 2 P.

Patt rows 3–8 Rep Rows 1 and 2 three times more.

Patt row 9 Sl 1, k3 [2; 1; 1], pick up the underlying thread and k1 st into it, k3, sl 1, k1, psso, *k2 tog, k3, (k1, p1) into the underlying thread, k3, sl 1, k1, psso; rep from * to last 9 [8, 7, 7] sts, k2 tog, k3, k1 st into the underlying thread, k4 [3, 2, 2].

Patt row 10 P.

Patt rows 11–16 Rep Rows 9 and 10 three times more.

The last 16 rows form the pattern used for the main part of the jumper; rep them until work measures 11½ [12, 12, 12¼]in (28.75 [29, 30, 31]cm).

SHAPE ARMHOLES

Next row Cast off 6 [7, 8, 9] sts at beginning of the next 2 rows (106 [112, 118, 126] sts), then dec 1 st at each end of every other row for 7 [9, 11, 13] times (92 [94, 96, 100] sts). Cont in patt until work measures 5 [5, 5½, 5¾]in (12.5 [12.5, 14, 14.5]cm) from start of armhole shaping.

A 17 (18, 19, 20)in
42.5 (45, 47.5, 50)cm

B 11½ (12, 12, 12¼)in
29 (30, 30, 31)cm

C 6½ (6½, 7, 7¼)in
16.5 (16.5, 17.5, 18)cm

D 13 (13½, 14, 14½)in
32.5 (34, 35, 36.5)cm

E 17½ (18, 18, 18¼)in
44 (45, 45, 46)cm

BACK NECK OPENING

Work 46 [47, 48, 50] sts in patt then sl rem 46 [47, 48, 50] sts onto a st-holder.

Cont without shaping in patt on the first set of sts for 1½in (4cm) more, ending with the yarn at the armhole edge.

SHAPE SHOULDERS

Cast off 5 [5, 5, 4] sts from the armhole edge in every other row 4 [4, 4, 6] times. Work 1 row and cast off 5 [5, 4, 4] sts. Work 1 row and cast off rem 26 [27, 28, 26] sts. Break yarn and rejoin it to neck opening edge of the other side and work to match first side.

FRONT

Work as for Back until piece measures 5 [5, 5½, 5¾]in (12.5 [12.5, 14, 14.5]cm) from the start of armhole shaping, ending on a RS row (92 [94, 96, 100] sts).

Next row (WS) Patt 34 [35, 36, 37] sts, loosely cast off 24 [24, 24, 26] sts, patt 34 [35, 36, 37] sts.

Now work one side of the neck at a time, dec 1 st at the neck edge every row for 5 [6, 6, 5] rows (29 [29, 30, 32] sts and then every other row 4 times (25 [25, 26, 28] sts.

Shape the shoulders as for the Back.

Rejoin the yarn to the neck edge of the other side and work to match first side.

SLEEVES (MAKE 2)

With 2.75mm needles and MC, cast on 40 [42, 44, 46] sts for the cuff, and work in k1, p1 rib for 4in (10cm). Now change to 3.75mm needles and work as follows:

Patt row 1 Sl 1, k4 [0, 1, 2], *k2 tog, k3, pick up the underlying thread between the st on the working needle and the next st to be worked, (k1, p1) into the picked-up thread (increasing 2 sts and forming a hole), k3, sl 1, k1, psso; rep from * to last 5 [1, 2, 3] sts, k5 [1, 2, 3].

Patt row 2 P.

Patt rows 3–8 Rep Rows 1 and 2 three times more.

Patt row 9 Sl 1, k4 [0, 1, 2], pick up the underlying thread and k1 st into it, k3, sl 1, k1, psso; *k2 tog, k3 (k1, p1) into the underlying thread, k3, sl 1, k1, psso; rep from * to last 10 [6, 7, 8] sts, k2 tog, k3, k1 st into the underlying thread, k5 [1, 2, 3].

Patt row 10 P.

Patt rows 11–16 Rep Rows 9 and 10 three times more.

When work measures 8 [8, 8¼, 8½]in (20 [20, 20.5, 21.5]cm), shape edges as follows:

Inc 1 st at each end of next and every following 6th row 5 times (50 [52, 54, 56] sts).

Inc 1 st at each end of every 4th row 10 times (70 [72, 74, 76] sts), then inc 1 st at each end of every row for 11 rows (92 [94, 96, 98] sts).

Inc 1 st at each end of every other row 8 times (108 [110, 112, 114] sts).

SHAPE SLEEVE CAP

Cast off 3 sts at beginning of every row for 13 rows (69 [71, 73, 75] sts), then dec 1 st at beginning of every row for 33 [33, 37, 39] rows. Cast off rem 36 [38, 40, 42] sts.

SCARF COLLAR

With 3.75mm needles and MC, cast on 3 sts and, working in moss-st, inc 1 st at beginning of every row to 65 sts.

Next row Work 24 sts in moss-st, loosely cast off 17 sts, work 24 sts moss-st. Now work one side at a time, *inc 1 st at outside edge in every 4th row and AT THE SAME TIME dec 1 st at the inside (neck) edge every other row until 20 sts rem.* Cont without shaping for 60 rows. Cast off.

Rejoin yarn to inside edge of other side and work from * to *. Cont without shaping for 36 rows. Cast off.

Now work another Scarf Collar exactly to match using CC.

MAKING UP

Press pieces lightly on WS using a warm iron over a damp cloth, taking care to avoid ribbed welts. Gather up about 5in (12.5cm) of the sleeve cap and tighten the gathering thread so that the sleeve top measures 3 1/2in (9cm) to give the fullness on the shoulders. Fasten off.

Join side and shoulder seams of jumper and sleeve seams, then stitch sleeves into armholes. Sew the buttons to the right-hand side of back opening, and to the left side crochet three button loops. Darn in ends.

Press the two scarf pieces and sew the CC scarf to the jumper neckline first, then the MC scarf on top. Make sure that the scarves don't lay exactly on top of each other (i.e. one has the short side to the left of the neck, the other has the short side to the right so that the two points have a space between them). Both scarf ends should sit either side of the back opening.

MAN'S CARDIGAN

Originally a fairly standard 1940s gent's cardigan, this version is given a luxuriously soft makeover using an alpaca/silk/cashmere yarn blend. Its versatility and generous fit will make it a wardrobe favourite in no time.

MATERIALS
Juno Alice Sock Yarn, 70% baby alpaca/ 20% silk/10% cashmere, 437yds (400m) per 100g ball as follows:

3 x 100g in Canopy (MC)

2 x 100g in Savannah (CC)

1 pair 3.25mm (US #3) needles

2 x 3.75mm (US #5) dpns

7 buttons

SIZING
TO FIT BUST SIZES
34in / 36in / 38in / 40in
(85cm / 90cm / 95cm / 100cm)

ACTUAL FINISHED MEASUREMENTS
Bust
40in / 42in / 44in / 46in
(100cm / 105cm / 110cm / 115cm)

Length (shoulder–hem)
24in / 24¾in / 26¼in / 27in
(60.5cm / 62cm / 65.5cm / 67.5cm)

Length (hem–underarm)
15½in / 16¼in / 17in / 17¾in
(39cm / 40.5cm / 42.5cm / 44.5cm)

Armhole depth
8½in / 8½in / 9¼in / 9¼in
(21.5cm / 21.5cm / 23cm / 23cm)

Shoulder to shoulder
14¾in / 15¾in / 17in / 18in
(37cm / 39cm / 42.5cm / 45cm)

Inner sleeve
18in / 18in / 18½in / 18½in
(45cm / 45cm / 46.5cm / 46.5cm)

TENSION
28 sts & 32 rows = 4in (10cm) using 3.25mm needles over main stitch.

ABBREVIATIONS
See page 11

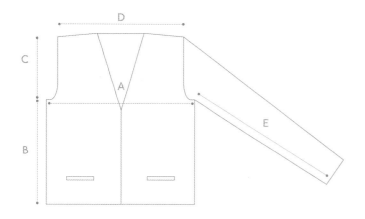

A 20 (21, 22, 23)in
   50 (52.5, 55, 57.5)cm

B 15½ (16¼, 17, 17¾)in
   39 (40.5, 42.5, 44.5)cm

C 8½ (8½, 9¼, 9¼)in
   21.5 (21.5, 23, 23)cm

D 14¾ (15¾, 17, 18)in
   37 (39.5, 42.5, 45)cm

E 18 (18, 18½, 18½)in
   45 (45, 46.5, 46.5)cm

PATTERN & STITCH NOTES

The cardigan is mostly knitted on dpns, ensuring that the correct yarn colour ends up at the correct side of the work.

The st patt rep is worked over 4 sts and 12 rows.

Sl all slipped sts purlwise. When casting off on patt rows for which sts have to be slipped to the other end of needle, cast the sts off first and replace the odd stitch onto left-hand needle before slipping sts to other end.

If you prefer working from a chart, use the chart on page 94 together with the written instructions.

DIRECTIONS

BACK

With 3.75mm dpns and MC, cast on 139 [147, 155, 163] sts and work 1in (2.5cm) in garter-st. Cont in patt as follows:

Row 1   (RS) With MC, k to end.

Row 2   With MC, p to end.

Row 3   With CC, *k3, sl 1; rep from
         * to last 3 sts, k3.
         Sl sts to other end of needle so
         that RS of work is still facing:

Row 4   With MC, k1, *sl 1, k3; rep from
         * to last 2 sts, sl 1, k1.

Row 5   With CC, *p3, sl 1; rep from
         * to last 3 sts, p3.
         Sl sts to other end of needle
         so that WS is still facing:

Row 6   With MC, p to end.

Row 7   With MC, k to end.

Row 8   With MC, p to end.

Row 9   With CC, k1, *sl 1, k3; rep from
         * to last 2 sts, sl 1, k1.
         Sl sts to other end of needle
         so that RS is still facing:

Row 10	With MC, *k3, sl 1; rep from * to last 3 sts, k3.
Row 11	With CC, p1, *sl 1, p3; rep from * to last 2 sts, sl 1, p1. Sl sts to other end of needle so that WS is still facing:
Row 12	With MC, p to end. These 12 rows form the patt.

Cont in patt until work measures 15½ [16¼, 17, 17¾]in (39 [40.5, 42.5, 44.5]cm), ending with a 6th or a 12th patt row.

SHAPE ARMHOLES
Keeping continuity of patt, cast off 4[4, 5, 5] sts at beginning of next 2 rows (131 [139, 145, 153] sts), then dec 1 st each end of every row until 103 [111, 119, 127] sts rem.

Cont without shaping until work measures 24 [24¾, 26¼, 27]in (60.5 [62, 65.5, 67.5]cm), ending with a 6th or a 12th patt row (WS row).

SHAPE SHOULDERS

Rows 1–2	Cast off 11 [12, 13, 13] sts, patt to end (81 [87, 93, 101] sts).
Rows 3–4	Cast off 11 [12, 12, 13] sts, patt to end (59 [63, 69, 75] sts).
Rows 5–6	Cast off 11 [11, 12, 13] sts, patt to end (37 [41, 45, 49] sts). Cast off rem 37 [41, 45, 49] sts.

RIGHT FRONT
Pocket lining
With 3.25mm needles and MC, cast on 35 sts and work 4in (10cm) in St-st, ending with a k (RS) row.

Leave sts on a st-holder.
With 3.75mm dpns and MC, cast on 75 [79, 83, 87] sts and work 1in (2.5cm) in garter-st.

Cont in patt with garter-st front border as follows:

Row 1	(RS) With MC, k to end.
Row 2	With MC, p to last 8 sts, k8.

Row 3	With MC, k8, change to CC, k3, *sl 1, k3; rep from * to end. Sl sts to other end of needle so that RS is still facing:
Row 4	With MC, sl 8, k1, *sl 1, k3; rep from * to last 2 sts, sl 1, k1.
Row 5	With CC, p3, *sl 1, p3; rep from * to last 8 sts, sl 8. Sl sts to other end of needle so that WS is still facing:
Row 6	With MC, p to last 8 sts, k8.
Row 7	With MC, k to end.
Row 8	With MC, p to last 8 sts, k8.
Row 9	With MC, k8, change to CC, k1, *sl 1, k3; rep from * to last 2 sts, sl 1, k1. Sl sts to other end of needle so that RS is still facing:
Row 10	With MC, sl 8, k3, *sl 1, k3; rep from * to end.
Row 11	With CC, p1, *sl 1, p3; rep from * to last 20 sts, sl 1, p1, sl 8. Sl sts to other end of needle so that WS is still facing:
Row 12	With MC, p to last 8 sts, k8. These 12 rows form the patt. Cont in patt until work measures approx 5in (12.5cm), ending with a 6th or a 12th patt row at the front edge (WS row).
Next row	With MC, k22 [24, 26, 28], k the next 35 sts and sl onto spare needle, k18 [20, 22, 24].
Next row	P18 [20, 22, 24], p across 35 sts of a pocket lining, p14 [16, 18, 20], k8 in MC.

Cont in patt with garter-st front border until work measures approx 15 [15¾, 16½, 17¼]in (37.5 [39.5, 41.5, 43]cm), ending at front edge with a 6th or a 12th patt row.

	SHAPE FRONT EDGE
Next row	With MC, k8, k2 tog, patt to end (74 [78, 82, 86] sts). Work 4 rows in patt, ending on a RS row (side edge).
	SHAPE ARMHOLE
Next row	Cast off 4 [4, 5, 5] sts, patt to last 8 sts, with MC k8 (70 [74, 77, 81] sts).
	Work 14 [14, 13, 13] rows in patt, dec 1 st at armhole edge on each row and AT THE SAME TIME dec 1 st at the front edge as before on next and every following 6th row (53 [57, 61, 65] sts). Now cont in patt with garter-st border, keeping the armhole edge straight and dec 1 st at the front edge as before on every 6th row until 41 [43, 45, 47] sts rem.
	Cont without shaping until work measures 24 [24¾, 26¼, 27]in (60.5 [62, 65.5, 67.5]cm), ending at armhole edge with a 7th or a 1st patt row (RS row).
	SHAPE SHOULDER
Row 1	Cast off 11 [12, 13, 13] sts, patt to end (30 [31, 32, 34] sts).
Row 2	Patt to end.
Row 3	Cast off 11 [12, 12, 13] sts, patt to end (19 [19, 20, 21] sts).
Row 4	Patt to end.
Row 5	Cast off 11 [11, 12, 13] sts, patt to end (8 sts).
Row 6	Patt to end. With MC, work in garter-st on rem 8 sts for 2½ [2¾, 3, 3¼]in (6.5 [7, 7.5, 8cm). Cast off.
	Place 7 pins in the right front border to mark position for buttons, the first one ¾ [½, ¾, ¼]in (2 [1.5, 2, 1]cm) from lower edge, the rest at 2¼ [2½, 2½, 2¾]in (5.5 [6.5, 6.5, 7]cm) intervals with the top one about ¾ [½,¾, ¼]in (2 [1.5, 2, 1]cm) below beginning of the front shaping.

LEFT FRONT

Work a pocket lining as given for the Right Front. With 3.75mm dpns and MC, cast on 75 [79, 83, 87] sts and work ¾in (2cm) in garter-st.

Next row	K3, cast off 3 sts for a buttonhole, k to end.
Next row	K to last 3 sts, cast on 3, k3. Cont in garter-st until work measures 1in (2.5cm), finishing with a row on WS at the side edge.
	Cont in patt with garter-st front border as follows:
Row 1	With MC, k to end.
Row 2	With MC, k8, p to end.
Row 3	With CC, k3, *sl 1, k3; rep from * to last 8 sts, sl 8. Sl sts to other end of needle so that RS is still facing:
Row 4	With MC, k1, *sl 1, k3; rep from * to last 10 sts, sl 1, k1, k8.
Row 5	With MC, k8, change to CC, p3, *sl 1, p3; rep from * to end. Sl sts back to other end of needle so that WS is still facing:
Row 6	With MC, sl 8, p to end.
Row 7	With MC, k to end.
Row 8	With MC, k8, p to end.
Row 9	With CC, k1, *sl 1, k3; rep from * to last 10 sts, sl 1, k1, sl 8. Sl sts back to other end of needle so that RS is still facing:
Row 10	With MC, k3, *sl 1, k3; rep from * to last 8 sts, k8.
Row 11	With MC, k8, change to CC, p1, *sl 1, p3; rep from * to last 2 sts, sl 1, p1. Sl sts back to other end of needle so that WS is still facing:

94

COLOURWORK AND STITCH PATTERN

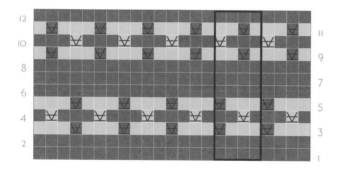

Key

■ MC (Canopy); k on RS, p on WS

□ CC (Savannah); k on RS, p on WS

Ⅴ Sl st purlwise on RS and WS

☐ Pattern repeat

Row 12	With MC, sl 8, p to end. These 12 rows form the patt.

Cont in patt, making further buttonholes as before in the garter-st front border at the points marked with pins in the right front border until work measures approx 5in (12.5cm), ending with a 6th or 12th patt row at the side edge (WS row).

Next row	K18 [20, 22, 24], k next 35 sts and slip onto st-holder, k22 [24, 26, 28] in MC.
Next row	With MC, k8, p22 [24, 26, 28], p across 35 sts for a pocket lining, p18 [20, 22, 24].

Cont in patt with garter-st front border and regular buttonholes until work is approx 15 [15¾, 16½, 17¼]in (37.5 [39.5, 41.5, 43]cm), ending with a 6th or a 12th patt row at the side edge (WS row) just after completing 7th buttonhole.

SHAPE FRONT EDGE

Next row	Patt to last 10 sts, k2 tog, k8 in MC (74 [78, 82, 86] sts). Work 5 rows in patt, ending on a WS row (side edge).

SHAPE ARMHOLE

Next row	Cast off 4 [4, 5, 5] sts, patt to last 10 sts, k2 tog, k8 in MC (69 [73, 76, 80] sts).

Work 14 [14, 13, 13] rows in patt, dec 1 st at armhole edge on each row and AT THE SAME TIME dec 1 st at the front edge as before on every following 6th row (53 [57, 61, 65] sts).
Now cont in patt with garter-st border, keeping armhole edge straight and dec 1 st at the front edge as before on every 6th row until 41 [43, 45, 47] sts rem.
Cont without shaping until work measures 24 [24¾, 26¼, 27]in (60.5 [62, 65.5, 67.5]cm), ending at armhole edge with a 6th or a 12th patt row (WS row).

SHAPE SHOULDER

Row 1	Cast off 11 [12, 13, 13] sts, patt to end (30 [31, 32, 34] sts).
Row 2	Patt to end.
Row 3	Cast off 11 [12, 12, 13] sts, patt to end (19 [19, 20, 21] sts).

Row 4	Patt to end.
Row 5	Cast off 11 [11, 12, 13] sts, patt to end (8 sts).
Row 6	Patt to end. With MC, work in garter-st on rem 8 sts for 2½ [2¾, 3, 3¼]in (6.5 [7, 7.5, 8cm). Cast off.

SLEEVES (MAKE 2)

With 3.25mm needles and MC, cast on 55 [55, 57, 57] sts and work 1in (2.5cm) in garter-st. Change to 3.75mm dpns and cont in patt as given for Back for 3in (7.5cm).

Keeping continuity of patt, inc 1 st at both ends of next row and of every following 5th row until there are 113 [113, 115, 115] sts on the needle. Cont without shaping until work measures 18 [18, 18½, 18½]in (45, 45, 46.5, 46.5] cm), or desired inner sleeve length, ending with a WS row.

SHAPE SLEEVE CAP

Dec 1 st at each end of every row until 93 [93, 95, 95] sts rem, then dec 1 st at each end of every other row until 73 [73, 75, 75] sts rem. Now dec 1 st at each end of every row until 53 [53, 55, 55] sts rem. Cast off.

POCKET BORDERS (MAKE 2)

Slip the 35 sts from st-holder onto a 3.25mm needle and, with MC, work 1in (2.5cm) in garter-st. Cast off.

MAKING UP

Pin the pieces out to the correct dimensions, then spray with water and allow to dry. Sew shoulder and side seams. Sew sleeve seams. Sew sleeves into armholes matching seams with side seams. Sew the cast-off edges of border together and sew this border along back of neck, making sure the seam matches the centre of Back. Stitch side edges of the pocket borders on RS and sew around pocket linings on WS. Sew on buttons to match with buttonholes. Darn in ends.

SPIRAL PATTERN JUMPER

This fantastic jumper from the 1930s encompasses knitting, crochet and simple embroidery. The crochet scarf (with embroidered squares) can be styled two ways. The close-fitting jumper has a shaped waist and is knitted using a simple 'wandering' cable pattern, while the welts are a simple knitted hem instead of the usual rib stitch.

MATERIALS

Jamieson & Smith 2-ply Jumper Weight, 100% Shetland wool, 125yds (115m) per 25g ball, as follows:

11 [11, 12, 12] x 25g in Shade #1284 (Heathered Tangerine) (MC)

5 x 25g in Shade #125 (Rust) (CC)

1 pair 3mm (US #2–3) needles

2 spare cable needles (dpns)

3.5mm (US #E/4) crochet hook

2 x 1in (25mm) buttons

1 x small button for the neck opening

SIZING

TO FIT SIZES
34in / 36in / 38in / 40in
(85cm / 90cm / 95cm / 100cm)

ACTUAL FINISHED MEASUREMENTS
Bust
34in / 36in / 38in / 40in
(85cm / 90cm / 95cm / 100cm)

Length (shoulder–hem)
20in / 20½in / 21½in / 22in
(50cm / 51.5cm / 54cm / 55cm)

Length (waist–underarm)
13½in / 14in / 14½in / 14½in
(34cm / 35cm / 36.5cm / 36.5cm)

Armhole depth
6½in / 6½in / 7in / 7½in
(16.5cm / 16.5cm / 17.5cm / 19cm)

Shoulder to shoulder
15in / 15½in / 16in / 16½in
(37.5cm / 39cm / 40cm / 41.5cm)

Inner sleeve
18in / 18in / 18½in / 18½in
(45cm / 45cm / 46.5cm / 46.5cm)

TENSION
32 sts & 40 rows = 4in (10cm) over unstretched main cable pattern.

ABBREVIATIONS
See page 11

See page 11

DIFFICULTY
+++++

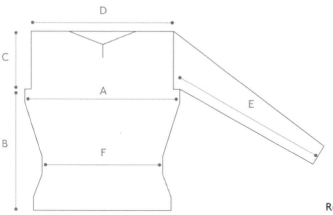

DIRECTIONS

FRONT

With MC, cast on 128 [132, 138, 144] sts and work in patt as follows:

Row 1   (RS) P1 [3, 5, 2], k1, p2, *k2, p5, k1, p4, k1, p2; rep from * 8 [8, 8, 9] times to last 4 [6, 8, 4] sts; k2, p2 [4, 6, 2].

Row 2   K2 [4, 6, 2], p2, *k2, p1, k4, p1, k5, p2; rep from * 8 [8, 8, 9] times to last 4 [6, 8, 5] sts; k2, p1, k1 [3, 5, 2].

Rows 3–10   Rep Rows 1 and 2 four times more.

Row 11   P1 [3, 5, 2], k1, p2, *sl the next 2 sts onto a spare needle and leave in front of work, p3 sts, k2 sts from spare needle, p2, k1, p4, k1, p2; rep from * 8 [8, 8, 9] times to last 4 [6, 8, 4] sts; k2, p2 [4, 6, 2].

Row 12   K2 [4, 6, 2], p2, *k2, p1, k4, p1, k2, p2, k3; rep from * 8 [8, 8, 9] times to last 4 [6, 8, 5] sts; k2, p1, k1 [3, 5, 2].

Row 13   P1 [3, 5, 2], k1, p2, *p3, k2, p2, k1, p4, k1, p2; rep from * 8 [8, 8, 9] times more to last 4 [6, 8, 4] sts; k2, p2 [4, 6, 2].

Row 14   Rep Row 12.

Rows 15–20   Rep Rows 13 and 14 three times more.

Row 21   P1 [3, 5, 2], k1, p2, *sl next 3 sts onto spare needle and leave at back of work, k2 sts, p3 sts from spare needle, p2, k1, p4, k1, p2; rep from * 8 [8, 8, 9] times more to last 4 [6, 8, 4] sts; k2, p2 [4, 6, 2].

Row 22   Rep Row 2.
Rows 2–22 form the patt and are repeated throughout the jumper.

Work 1.5in (4cm) in patt without shaping, then start decreasing for waist shaping as follows, keeping in patt throughout:

Dec 1 st at beginning of next 2 rows (126 [130, 136, 142] sts).

A   17 (18, 19, 20)in
    42.5 (45, 47.5, 50)cm

B   13½ (14, 14½, 14½)in
    34 (35, 36.5, 36.5)cm

C   6½ (6½, 7, 7½)in
    16.5 (16.5, 17.5, 19)cm

D   15 (15½, 16, 16½)in
    37.5 (39, 40, 41.5)cm

E   18 (18, 18½, 18½)in
    45 (45, 46.5, 46.5)cm

F   14¾ (15¼, 16, 16¾)in
    37 (38, 40, 42)cm

*Work 4 rows without shaping, then dec 1 st at beginning of next 2 rows. Rep from * 3 times more (118 [122, 128, 134] sts).

Work 28 rows without shaping. Start increasing for bust shaping as follows:

Row 1   Inc 1 st at each end of row.

Rows 2–6   Work 5 rows in patt without shaping (120 [124, 130, 136] sts).

Row 7   Inc 1 st at each end of row.

Rows 8–10   Work 3 rows in patt without shaping (122 [126, 132, 138] sts).

Row 11   Inc 1 st at each end of row.

Rows 12–16   Work 5 rows in patt without shaping. Rep Rows 7–16 until 136 [144, 152, 160] sts are on needle.

Cont straight until work measures 13 1/2 [14, 14 1/2, 14 1/2]in (34 [35, 36.5, 36.5]cm).

SHAPE ARMHOLE
Cast off 5 [6, 7, 7] sts at beginning of next 2 rows for the armholes (126 [132, 138, 146] sts).

Dec 1 st each end of every other row until 120 [124, 128, 132] sts rem.

Cont working in patt without shaping until work measures 2 1/2 [2 1/2, 3, 3 1/2]in (6.5 [6.5, 7.5, 9]cm) from beginning of armhole shaping.

SHAPE RIGHT NECK
Next row   Work across 60 [62, 64, 66] sts and leave these sts on a st-holder, then work a further 2in (5cm) from beginning of split on the rem 60 [62, 64, 66] sts without shaping, ending with a WS row.

Next row   *Cast off 4 sts (neck edge), work to end of row (56 [58, 60, 62] sts).

Next row   Work without shaping. Rep last 2 rows twice more (48 [50, 52, 54] sts).

Next row   Cast off 3 sts, work to end of row (45 [47, 49, 51] sts).

Next row   Work without shaping. Rep last 2 rows once more (42 [44, 46, 48] sts).

Next row   Cast off 2 sts, work to end of row (40 [42, 44, 46] sts).

Next row   Work without shaping. Rep last 2 rows 2 [3, 2, 1] more times (36 [36, 40, 44] sts).

Work without shaping until armhole measures 6 1/2 [6 1/2, 7, 7 1/2]in (16.5 [16.5, 17.5, 19]cm) from beginning of shaping.

Cast off rem sts*.

SHAPE LEFT NECK
Return to rem 60 [62, 64, 66] sts for the Left Front.

Join yarn to neck edge (WS), cast on 4 sts for button band and work to end of row (64 [66, 68, 70] sts).

Next row   (RS) Work in patt to last 4 sts, k4.

Next row   K4, work in patt to end of row. Rep last 2 rows, working a further 2in (5cm) from beginning of split without shaping to match the straight Right-Hand Neck section, ending on RS row.

Next row   (WS) Cast off 4 sts (neck edge), work to end of row.

Now rep instructions for the Right-Hand Neck Shaping from * to *, making the shaping at beginning of the WS rows (i.e. the neck edge).

BACK
With MC, cast on 128 [132, 138, 144] sts and work in patt, working the shapings as for Front until sts have been cast off and decreased for the armholes (120 [124, 128, 132] sts).

Cont in patt without shaping until armhole measures 6 1/2 [6 1/2, 7, 7 1/2]in (16.5 [16.5, 17.5, 19]cm). Cast off.

SLEEVES (MAKE 2)

With MC, cast on 51 [51, 55, 55] sts
and work in patt as follows:

Row 1 (RS) *K1, p4, k1, p2, k2, p5; rep from *
twice more to last 6 [6, 10, 10] sts; k1,
p4, k1, p0 [0, 4, 4].

Row 2 K0 [0, 4, 4], p1, k4, p1, *k5, p2, k2, p1, k4,
p1; rep from * to end of row.
Rep last two rows until work measures
1in (2.5cm) from cast-on edge (this
forms the hem).

Now cont in main patt until work
measures 2½in (6.5cm).

Cont in patt, inc 1 st at each end of
every 8th row until 87 [87, 89, 95] sts
are on needle.

Cont to work without further shaping
until sleeve measures 18 [18, 18½, 18½]in
(45 [45, 46.5, 46.5]cm) from cast-on edge.

SHAPE SLEEVE CAP

Cast off 6 [6, 5, 5] sts at beginning
of next 2 rows (75 [75, 79, 85] sts).

Dec 1 st at each end of every other row
until 27 [27, 31, 35] sts rem. Cast off 3
sts at beginning of next 4 rows (15 [15,
19, 23] sts).

Cast off 2 sts at beginning of next
2 rows (11 [11, 15, 19] sts).

Cast off rem sts.

SCARF

The scarf is written in UK crochet terms
with the US equivalent in brackets. This
is worked entirely in CC using dc (sc)
and tr (dc) crochet. With CC, make 190
ch rather loosely.

Row 1 Work 1 tr (dc) into 3rd ch from hook,
1 tr (dc) into next stitch, *1 dc (sc) into
each of the next 2 sts and 1 tr (dc) into
each of the next 2 sts; rep from * to
end, finishing with 2 tr (dc), 1 ch. Turn.

Row 2 Work 2 tr (dc) over the 2 dc (sc), then
2 dc (sc) over the 2 tr (dc) of the last
row, dec in the middle of the work by
skipping 2 sts and AT THE SAME TIME dec 1
st at each end of the work every row.

Cont working in this manner, loosely,
and working into both loops of the sts
until 2in (5cm) have been worked.

Form two buttonholes at both ends
as follows: work in patt for 2in (5cm),
*ch 2 sts, skip 2 sts from previous
row*, cont in patt until 2in (5cm) from
edge of work. Rep from * to * to form
another buttonhole, patt to end.
Cont in patt, remembering to dec
1 st at both ends of work and 2 sts
at centre until 86 sts remain, then
fasten off.

With MC and a darning needle, darn
in little squares all over the scarf at
even intervals. Work a diagonal line
of running stitch across each long
bottom corner approx 5in (12.5cm)
in from the point and draw up,
forming 'ears'.

MAKING UP

Press pieces lightly on WS using a
warm iron over a damp cloth. At the
wrist edge of each sleeve, turn up a
1in (2.5cm) hem and stitch down lightly
on WS. Sew shoulder and side seams
of jumper. Sew sleeve seams, then
sew sleeves into armholes. Sew small
button to left side of front opening
and crochet a small buttonhole
loop to correspond on right side.
Sew buttons onto jumper as shown
in illustration and arrange scarf as
desired. Darn in ends.

TRICOLOUR PULLOVER

The 1950s were all about emphasizing the waist, and this pattern is a prime example – the voluminous three-quarter-length batwing sleeves are knitted from the top down and shaped using short rows, while the geometric colour scheme gives it a somewhat Swiss 'bib' appearance.

MATERIALS
Our pullover was knitted with Rowan Cashsoft, now discontinued.
This alternative will knit to the same tension and sizing. Rowan Pure Wool 4-ply 100% wool, 174yds (160m) per 50g ball, as follows:

4 [5, 5, 5] x 50g Shade #402 (Shale) (A)

2 [2, 3, 3] x 50g Shade #410 (Indigo) (B)

5 [6, 6, 6] x 50g Shade #451 (Porcelaine) (C)

1 pair 2.25mm (US #1) needles

1 pair 2.75mm (US #2) needles

3 buttons

SIZING
TO FIT BUST SIZES
34in / 36in / 38in / 40in
(85cm / 90cm / 95cm / 100cm)

ACTUAL FINISHED MEASUREMENTS
Bust
34in / 36in / 38in / 40in
(85cm / 90cm / 95cm / 100cm)

Length (shoulder–hem)
19½in / 20½in / 21½in / 22½in
(49cm / 51.5cm / 54cm / 56.5cm)

Length (hem–underarm)
8in / 8½in / 9in / 9½in
(20cm / 21.5cm / 22.5cm / 24cm)

Armhole depth
11½in / 12in / 12½in / 13in
(29cm / 30cm / 31.5cm / 32.5cm)

Shoulder to shoulder
12in / 13in / 14in / 15in
(30cm / 32.5cm / 35cm / 37.5cm)

Inner sleeve
16in / 16in / 16½in / 16½in
(40cm / 40cm / 41.5cm / 41.5cm)

TENSION
28 sts & 40 rows = 4in (10cm) using 2.75mm needles over Stocking stitch.

ABBREVIATIONS
See page 11

DIFFICULTY
+++++

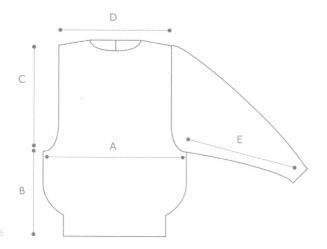

A 17 (18, 19, 20)in
   42.5 (45, 47.5, 50)cm

B 8 (8½, 9, 9½)in
   20 (21.5, 22.5, 24)cm

C 11½ (12, 12½, 13)in
   29 (30, 31.5, 32.5)cm

D 12 (13, 14, 15)in
   30 (32.5, 35, 37.5)cm

E 16 (16, 16½, 16½)in
   40 (40, 41.5, 41.5)cm

DIRECTIONS

BACK

With 2.25mm needles and A, cast on
98 [106, 112, 120] sts. Work in k1, p1 rib
for 3in (7.5cm).

Next row (WS) Rib 5 [9, 6, 5], *inc 1, rib 7 [7, 8, 9];
rep from * to last 6 [10, 8, 6] sts, inc 1,
rib to end (110 [118, 124, 132] sts).

Change to 2.75mm needles. Cont
in St-st and inc 1 st at each end of 7th
row and every following 6th row 4
[3, 4, 3] times (120 [126, 134, 140] sts).
Cont without shaping until work
measures 8 [8½, 9, 9½]in (20 [21.5, 22.5,
24]cm), ending with a WS row.

SHAPE ARMHOLE

Cast off 11 sts at beginning of next
2 rows (98 [104, 112, 118] sts).

Dec 1 st at each end of every third row
7 [6, 7, 6] times (84 [92, 98, 106] sts).
Work even until armhole measures 3½
[4, 4½, 4½]in (9 [10, 11.5, 11.5]cm), ending
with a WS row.

YOKE

Row 1 K21 [23, 24, 27] in A, attach C, k42
[46, 50, 52] in C, attach A, k21
[23, 24, 27] in A.

Row 2 P21 [23, 24, 27] in A, p42 [46, 50, 52]
in C, p21 [23, 24, 27] in A.

Row 3 K20 [22, 23, 26] in A, k44 [48, 52, 54]
in C, k20 [22, 23, 26] in A.

Row 4 P20 [22, 23, 26] in A, p44 [48, 52, 54]
in C, p20 [22, 23, 26] in A.

Cont as above, adding 2 more sts in
C at centre on every RS (k) row until
all sts are worked with C. Break A.
Cont without shaping in C until back
measures 17½ [18½, 19½, 20½]in
(44 [46, 49, 51.5]cm) from cast-on
edge, ending with a WS row.

BACK OPENING

Next row K45 [49, 52, 56] sts, turn.
Place rem sts on st-holder.

Next row	K6, p to end. Cont on 45 [49, 52, 56] sts and work 6 sts in garter-st at inner edge until work measures 19½ [20½, 21½, 22½]in (49 [51.5, 54, 56.5]cm) from cast-on edge, ending at armhole edge.

SHAPE SHOULDERS

Cast off 11 [12, 13, 14] sts at beginning of next and following alt row. Work 1 row. Cast off rem 23 [25, 26, 28] sts for back neck. With pins, mark for 3 buttons evenly spaced along garter-st edge.

With RS facing, rejoin yarn to other side and cast on 6 sts, then k across 6 sts just cast on and rem 39 [43, 46, 50] sts from holder. Complete to match other side, working 3 buttonholes opposite markers in garter-st edge as follows:

Buttonhole	K2, cast off 2 sts, k2, work to end. On next row, cast on 2 sts over cast-off sts.

FRONT

Work exactly as for Back until work measures 18 [18½, 19, 20]in (45 [46, 47.5, 50]cm), ending with a WS row.

SHAPE NECK

Next row	K30 [34, 37, 41] sts, turn. Leave rem sts on a st-holder. Dec 1 st at neck edge on every other row until 22 [24, 26, 28] sts remain. Cont without shaping until work measures 19½ [20 1/2, 21½, 22½] in (49 [51.5, 54, 56.5]cm) from cast-on edge, ending at armhole edge.

SHAPE SHOULDERS

Cast off 11 [12, 13, 14] sts at beginning of next row. Work 1 row, cast off rem sts. With RS facing, cast off the centre 24 sts, then k to end. Complete to match first side, reversing shapings.

SLEEVES (MAKE 2)

The sleeves are worked from the top down.

With 2.75mm needles and B, and RS facing, pick up and k 160 [166, 174, 180] sts around armhole edge. Work in k1, p1 rib for 2in (5cm), ending with a WS row. Break B. Attach C and cont in St-st. Work 10 rows straight.

Row 11	K78 [81, 85, 88], (k2 tog) twice, k to end (158 [164, 172, 178] sts). Work 5 rows.
Row 17	K2 tog, k75 [78, 82, 85], (k2 tog) twice, k to last 2 sts, k2 tog (154 [160, 168, 174] sts.
Row 18	P.
Next 2 rows	Work to last 20 sts, w&t. P next row.
Next 2 rows	Work to last 25 sts, w&t. P next row.
Next 2 rows	Work to last 5 sts of turning on last row, w&t. Rep last 2 rows, knitting 5 sts fewer on every row until there are 30 [36, 44, 50] sts between last 2 turnings.
Next row	(RS) K across all sts.
Next row	P across all sts. Cont without turning, dec 1 st at each end of every other row until 144 [150, 158, 164] sts rem. P1 row.
Next 2 rows	Work to within last 15 sts, w&t.
Next 2 rows	Work to within last 20 sts, w&t. Rep last 2 rows, knitting 5 sts fewer on every row until there are 42 [48, 56, 62] sts on needle between last 2 turnings, w&t.
Next row	K across all sts.
Next row	P across all sts. Cont without turning, decreasing 1 st at each end of every other row until 134 [140, 148, 154] sts remain. P1 row.
Next 2 rows	Work to within last 15 sts, w&t.
Next 2 rows	Work to within last 20 sts, w&t. Rep last 2 rows, knitting 5 sts fewer on every row until there are 44 [50, 58, 64] sts on needle between last 2 turnings, w&t.
Next row	K across all sts.

Next row	P across all sts.

Cont without turning, dec 1 st at each end of every other row until 116 [122, 130, 136] sts rem. Dec 1 st at each end of every other row 14 times (88 [94, 102, 108] sts), then dec 1 st at each end of every row until 56 sts rem, ending with a WS row. Break C. Attach A and k 2 rows. Break A and attach B. Change to 2.25mm needles and work in St-st for 1in (2.5cm), ending with a RS row.

Next row (WS) K to end (forming the hemline). Cont in St-st for 1in (2.5cm). Cast off loosely.

MAKING UP
Neckband
Press pieces lightly on WS using a warm iron over a damp cloth. Sew shoulder seams. With C and 2.25mm needles, and RS facing, pick up and k 110 [114, 116, 120] sts around neck edge. Work in St-st for 1/2in (1.5cm), ending with a k row. K1 row (hemline). Cont in St-st for 1/2in (1.5cm). Cast off loosely.

Sew side and sleeve seams. Sew sleeves into armholes. Turn under hems on cuffs and neckband and sew in place. Slip stitch underlap in place at back neck opening. Sew on buttons. Darn in ends.

TUCK-IN SURPLICE

IIO

An elegant 1950s pattern. We've worked this wrapover surplice in black to lend it an evening blazer look. The shoulders have a pin-tuck at the outer edges to give a boxier silhouette, while the elasticated waist is secured with two buttons. The stitch is simple, but it takes a little time to work up – the result is so stylish we think it's worth it.

MATERIALS

Wollmeise Twin Sock Yarn, 80% merino wool/20% polyamid, 510yds (466m) per 150g ball, as follows:

3 x 150g in Black

I pair 3.25mm (US #3) needles

2.25mm (US #B/I) crochet needle

2 buttons

30 [31½, 33, 34½]in (75 [79, 82.5, 86]cm) x Iin (2.5cm) wide elastic

SIZING

TO FIT BUST SIZES
34in / 36in / 38in / 40in
(85cm / 90cm / 95cm / 100cm)

ACTUAL FINISHED MEASUREMENTS
Bust
34in / 36in / 38in / 40in
(85cm / 90cm / 95cm / 100cm)

Length (shoulder–hem)
17½in / 18¼in / 19in / 20¼in
(44cm / 46cm / 47.5cm / 50.5cm)

Length (hem–underarm)
IIin / II½in / 12in / 13in
(27.5cm / 29cm / 30cm / 32.5cm)

Armhole depth
6½in / 6¾in / 7in / 7¼in
(16.5cm / 17cm / 17.5cm / 18cm)

Shoulder to shoulder
IIin / II½in / 12in / 12½in
(27.5cm / 29cm / 30cm / 31.5cm)

Inner sleeve
4in / 4½in / 5in / 5in
(10cm / 11.5cm / 12.5cm / 12.5cm)

TENSION

40 sts & 40 rows = 4in (10cm) over stitch pattern.

ABBREVIATIONS

See page II

DIFFICULTY
++++ +

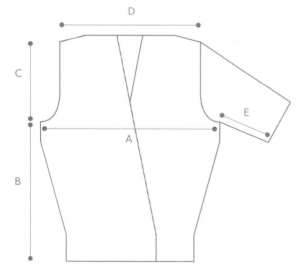

A   17 (18, 19, 20)in
    42.5 (45, 47.5, 50)cm

B   11 (11½, 12, 13)in
    27.5 (29, 30, 32.5)cm

C   6½ (6¾, 7, 7¼)in
    16.5 (17, 17.5, 18)cm

D   11 (11½, 12, 12½)in
    27.5 (29, 30, 31.5)cm

E   4 (4½, 5, 5)in
    10 (11.5, 12.5, 12.5)cm

DIRECTIONS

BACK

Cast on 130 [136, 142, 148] sts
and work in patt as follows:

Row 1 *K2 tog, keep sts on left-hand needle,
and k into back of same 2 sts; rep from
* to end.

Row 2 *K1, p1; rep from * to end.

Rep last 2 rows for patt. Cont in patt
without shaping until work measures
3 [3½, 4, 4]in (7.5 [9, 10, 10]cm).
Inc 1 st in each of first 2 and last 2 sts
of next row and every 7th row, until
there are 170 [180, 190, 200] sts. Work
even until piece measures 11[11½, 12, 13]
in (27.5 [29, 30, 32.5]cm).

SHAPE ARMHOLES

Cast off 8 sts at beginning of next
2 rows (154 [164, 174, 184]sts). Cast off
2 sts at beginning of next 4 rows (146
[156, 166, 176] sts). Dec 1 st at each end
of every row until 140 [146, 152, 158]
sts rem. Cont without shaping until
armhole measures 6½ [6¾, 7, 7¼]in
(16.5 [17, 17.5, 18]cm).

SHAPE SHOULDERS

Cast off 8 sts at beginning of next
10 rows. Cast off rem 60 [66, 72, 78]
sts for back neck.

RIGHT FRONT

Cast on 86 [90, 94, 98] sts and work
in patt for 6 rows, then work 2
buttonholes as follows:

**Buttonhole
row 1** Work 4 sts in patt, cast off 3 sts, work
in patt over next 18 sts, cast off 3 sts,
work to end.

**Buttonhole
row 2** Work in patt across and cast on 3 sts
over cast-off sts.

Cont in patt until work measures
3 [3½, 4, 4]in (7.5 [9, 10, 10]cm), ending
with 2nd patt row. Inc 1 st in each of
last 2 sts at side edge on next row and
every 7th row until there are 104 [108,
112, 116] sts. Cont without shaping until

work measures 11[11½, 12, 13]in (27.5 [29, 30, 32.5]cm), ending at side edge.

SHAPE ARMHOLE

Cast off 8 sts at beginning of next row. Cast off 2 sts at same edge every other row 2 times. Dec 1 st at armhole edge on every row until 84 [86, 88, 90] sts rem. Cont without shaping until armhole measures 6½ [6 3/4, 7, 7¼]in (16.5 [17, 17.5, 18]cm), ending at armhole edge.

SHAPE SHOULDER

Row 1   Cast off 24 sts.

Row 2   Patt to end.

Row 3   Cast off 8 sts, patt to end.

Row 4   Patt to end.

Rows 5–10   Rep Rows 3 and 4 three more times. Work in patt over rem 28 [30, 32, 34] sts for collar, until piece fits across to centre back neck.

LEFT FRONT

Work to match Right Front, reversing shapings and omitting buttonholes.

SLEEVES (MAKE 2)

Cast on 110 [114, 118, 122] sts. Work in patt and inc 1 st in each of first 2 and last 2 sts of every 6th row until there are 126 [130, 134, 138] sts. Cont in patt without shaping until work measures 4 [4½, 5, 5]in (10 [11.5, 12.5, 12.5]cm).

SHAPE SLEEVE CAP

Cast off 8 sts at beginning of next 2 rows (110 [114, 118, 122] sts). Dec 1 st at each end of next 2 rows. Work 2 rows straight without shaping. Rep last 4 rows 4 [5, 6, 7] times more (90 [90, 90, 90] sts). Dec 1 st at each end of every row until 22 [24, 26, 28] sts rem. Cast off.

MAKING UP

Do not press. Sew side seams. Make a pleat at shoulder edge of each front, by placing a pin at 16th and 24th sts in from armhole edge. Fold 16th st over to armhole edge to form pleat and sew down for 4in (10cm), parallel to armhole edge along 24th st. Sew shoulder and sleeve seams. Sew in sleeves. Sew collar seams. Work a row of dc (sc) closely along lower edge of blouse. Cross-stitch elastic to inside of blouse at waist edge. Sew on buttons to correspond with buttonholes. Darn in ends.

A TWINSET IN SIMPLE STITCHES
(A DUET IN KNITTING)

We've worked this gorgeous 1940s twinset in shocking pink and burnt orange for a modern contrast. Both garments are mainly knitted in a rib stitch, which gives elasticity and a close fit, with 'fancy stitch' pattern panels. The short-sleeved jumper uses the panel to great effect on the sleeves and yoke, and easy-to-crochet buttons add a nice finish.

CARDIGAN

MATERIALS
Cascade 220 Fingering, 100% Peruvian Highland wool, 273yds (250m) per 50g ball, as follows:

6 [6, 7, 7] x 50g in Shade #7802 (Cerise)

1 pair 3.25mm (US #3) needles

2.25mm (US #B/1) crochet hook

SIZING
TO FIT BUST SIZES
34in / 36in / 38in / 40in
(85cm / 90cm / 95cm / 100cm)

ACTUAL FINISHED MEASUREMENTS
(OVER UNSTRETCHED RIB)
Bust
21in / 23in / 25in / 27in
(52.5cm / 57.5cm / 62.5cm / 67.5cm)

Length (shoulder–hem)
20½in / 20½in / 21in / 21in
(51.5cm / 51.5cm / 52.5cm / 52.5cm)

Length (hem–underarm)
13¾in / 13¾in / 14in / 14in
(34.5cm / 34.5cm / 35cm / 35cm)

Armhole depth
6¾in / 6¾in / 7in / 7in
(17cm / 17cm / 17.5cm / 17.5cm)

Shoulder to shoulder
13in / 14in / 14½in / 15in
(32.5cm / 35cm / 36.5cm / 37.5cm)

Inner sleeve
17½in / 18in / 18in / 18¼in
(44cm / 45cm / 45cm / 45.5cm)

TENSION
32 sts & 40 rows = 4in (10cm)
over slightly stretched k2, p2 rib.

ABBREVIATIONS
See page 11

DIFFICULTY
+++++

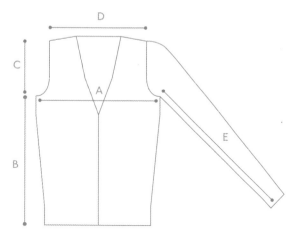

CARDIGAN

A 10½ (11½, 12½, 13½)in
    26.5 (29, 31.5, 34)cm

B 13¾ (13¾, 14, 14)in
    34.5 (34.5, 35, 35)cm

C 6¾ (6¾, 7, 7)in
    17 (17, 17.5, 17.5)cm

D 13 (14, 14½, 15)in
    32.5 (35, 36.5, 37.5)cm

E 17½ (18, 18, 18¼)in
    44 (45, 45, 45.5)cm

CARDIGAN DIRECTIONS

BACK
Cast on 104 [112, 120, 128] sts.
Work in k2, p2 rib, but with an
odd st at each end as follows:

Row 1 *P1, k2, p1; rep from * to end.

Row 2 *K1, p2, k1; rep from * to end.
Cont until work measures 4½in (11.5cm),
then inc 1 st at each end of next and
every following 4th row to 140 [148,
156, 164] sts. Cont without shaping
until work measures 13¾ [13¾, 14,
14]in (34.5 [34.5, 35, 35]cm).

SHAPE ARMHOLES
Cast off 4 sts at beginning of next
6 rows (116 [124, 132, 140] sts).

Dec 1 st at each end of next 6 [6, 8,
10] rows (104 [112, 116, 120] sts). Cont
straight until armhole measures 6¾
(6¾, 7, 7)in (17 [17, 17.5, 17.5]cm), finishing
on a WS row.

SHAPE SHOULDERS
Cast off 8 [9, 10, 8] sts at beginning
of next 2 rows (88 [94, 96, 104] sts).

Cast off 8 [9, 7, 8] sts at beginning
of next 6 rows (40 [40, 54, 56] sts).

Cast off 0 [0, 7, 8] sts at beginning
of next 2 rows.

Cast off rem 40 sts.

RIGHT FRONT
Cast on 70 [74, 78, 82] sts. Work
the 12 front edge sts in k1, p1 rib, then
the next 19 sts in fancy pattern, and
rem sts in rib as for Back as follows:

Row 1 (P1, k1) 6 times, p19, *k2, p2;
rep from * to last st, p1.

Row 2 Rib 39 [43, 47, 51] sts, k19, (p1, k1) 6 times.

Row 3 (P1, k1) 6 times, then work first row
of fancy pattern over next 19 sts
as follows:

(P1, p2 tog, yrn, p1, yrn, p4, p3 tog, p4,
yrn, p1, yrn, p2 tog, p1), rib to end.

Row 4	Rib 39 [43, 47, 51] sts, (k1, k2 tog, yf, k1, yf, k4, k3 tog, k4, yf, k1, yf, k2 tog, k1), (p1, k1) 6 times.
Row 5	Rep Row 3.
Row 6	Rep Row 4.
Row 7 (Buttonhole)	*(P1, k1) 3 times, cast off 2, (p1, k1) twice *, then as for Row 3.
Row 8 (Buttonhole)	Rep Row 4 until last 10 rib sts, then *rib 4, cast on 2, rib 6*.
Row 9	(P1, k1) 6 times, (p3, p2 tog, p4, yrn, p1, yrn, p4, p2 tog, p3), rib to end.
Row 10	Rib 39 [43, 47, 51] sts, (k3, k2 tog, k4, yf, k1, yf, k4, k2 tog, k3), rib 12.
Rows 11–14	Rep Rows 9 and 10 twice. Rep from Row 3 to Row 14 inclusive for each repetition of the pattern, and work 3 more buttonholes (as instructed from * to * in Rows 7 & 8) every 2 1/4in (5.5cm). When work measures 4 1/2in (11.5cm), inc 1 st at side edge on next and every following 4th row to 88 [92, 96, 100] sts. When 4th buttonhole has been worked, start dec for neck shaping, as follows:

NECK SHAPING

Next row	(P1, k1) over 12 sts, work 19 sts of fancy pattern, k2 tog, cont in rib pattern to end of row.

Rep this dec row on every following 8th row until 8 sts have been decreased AT THE SAME TIME as you are making the neck shaping, start shaping armhole when side seam measures the same as Back to armhole, as follows:

SHAPE ARMHOLE

Cast off 4 sts at beginning of next 4 rows at side edge, then dec 1 st at same side on next 10 [14, 16, 18] rows.

Cont with armhole side straight until neck shaping is finished, then cont without shaping on rem 54 [54, 56, 58] sts until armhole measures 7 1/4 [7 1/4, 7 1/2, 7 1/2]in (18 [18, 19, 19]cm).

SHAPE SHOULDER

Row 1	Cast off 10 [10, 12, 14] sts, patt to end (44 sts).
Row 2	Patt to end.
Row 3	Cast off 10 sts, patt to end (34 sts).
Rows 4–5	Rep Rows 2 & 3 (24 sts).
Row 6	Rep Row 2. Cast off 12 sts, leaving 12 sts at the neck edge. Work in k1, p1 rib over these 12 sts for a depth of 2 1/2in (6.5cm). Cast off.

LEFT FRONT

Work as for Right Front, with the front border and all shapings at opposite edges and omitting buttonholes.

SLEEVES (MAKE 2)

Cast on 52 [52, 54, 56] sts and work in k2, p2 rib as for Back. Work 4 rows, then inc 1 st at each end of next and every following 6th row to 84 [84, 86, 88] sts. Work 3 rows without shaping, then inc 1 st at each end of next and every following 4th row to 110 [110, 112, 114] sts. Cont without shaping until work measures 17 1/2 [18, 18, 18 1/4]in (44 [45, 45, 45.5]cm), or desired length to underarm.

SHAPE SLEEVE CAP

Next row	K2 tog at each end of every 3rd row until 88 [88, 90, 92] sts rem, then k2 tog at each end of every other row until 60 [60, 62, 64] sts rem.

Cast off 2 sts at beginning of next 4 rows (52 [52, 54, 56] sts).

Cast off.

MAKING UP

Do not press. Bear in mind when you're stitching the garment together that the rib stitch is used to create a flexible fabric — there will be areas where you need to allow for that flexibility and let the fabric stretch. Sew the shoulders together, easing in the extra sts of the fronts. Join the neck borders and stitch to the back of the neck. Make a pleat on the top of each sleeve, then sew the tops of the sleeves into the armholes. Press the work lightly on the wrong side with a hot iron over a damp cloth. Sew up the side and sleeve seams and press these. Darn in ends.

BUTTONS

Work 4 ch and join into a ring.

Next row Work 3 ch, then 15 tr (dc) into the ring, join by a sl st to the top of the 3 ch at the beginning.

Next row Work 1 dc (sc) into the top of each tr (dc).

Gather round the tops of the dc (sc), stuff with odd bits of the wool, draw up and stitch. Make 3 more buttons in the same way. Stitch these to the left front border to correspond with the buttonholes.

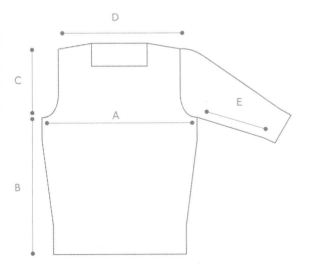

JUMPER

MATERIALS

Cascade 220 Fingering, 100% Peruvian Highland wool, 273yds (250m) per 50g ball, as follows:

5 [5, 6, 6] x 50g in Shade #7824 (Burnt Orange)

1 pair 3.25mm (US #3) needles

2.25mm (US #B/1) crochet hook

SIZING

TO FIT BUST SIZES
34in / 36in / 38in / 40in
(85cm / 90cm / 95cm / 100cm)

ACTUAL FINISHED MEASUREMENTS
(OVER UNSTRETCHED RIB)
Bust
18½in / 20½in / 22½in / 24½in
(46.5cm / 51.5cm / 56.5cm / 61.5cm)

Length (shoulder–hem)
19in / 19½in / 20in / 20¼in
(48cm / 49cm / 50cm / 50.5cm)

Length (hem–underarm)
12½in / 13in / 13in / 13in
(31.5cm / 32.5cm / 32.5cm / 32.5cm)

Armhole depth
6½in /6½in / 7in / 7¼in
(16.5cm / 16.5cm / 17.5cm / 18cm)

Shoulder to shoulder
13in / 14in / 14¾in / 15½in
(32.5cm / 35cm / 37cm / 39cm)

Inner sleeve
6¾in / 6¾in / 6¾in / 6¾in
(17cm / 17cm / 17cm / 17cm)

TENSION

32 sts & 40 rows = 4in (10cm) over slightly stretched k2, p2 rib.

ABBREVIATIONS
See page 11

123

JUMPER

A 9¼ (10¼, 11¼, 12¼)in
   23.5 (26, 28, 31)cm

B 12½ (13, 13, 13)in
   31.5 (32.5, 32.5, 32.5)cm

C 6½ (6½, 7, 7¼)in
   16.5 (16.5, 17.5, 18)cm

D 13 (14, 14¾, 15½)in
   32.5 (35, 37, 39)cm

E 6¾ (6¾, 6¾, 6¾)in
   17 (17, 17, 17)cm

JUMPER DIRECTIONS

BACK

Cast on 104 [112, 120, 128] sts. Work in k2, p2 rib, but with an odd st at each end as follows:

Row 1 *P1, k2, p1; rep from * to end.

Row 2 *K1, p2, k1; rep from * to end.
Cont until work measures 3½in (9cm), then inc at each end of next and every following 4th row to 140 [148, 156, 164] sts. Cont without shaping until work measures 12½ [13, 13, 13]in (31.5 [32.5, 32.5, 32.5]cm).

SHAPE ARMHOLES

Cast off 4 [4, 5, 6] sts at beginning of next 6 rows (116 [124, 126, 128] sts).

Dec 1 st at each end of next 6 [6, 4, 2] rows (104 [112, 118, 124] sts). Cont straight until armhole measures 6½ [6½, 7, 7¼]in (16.5 [16.5, 17.5, 18]cm), ending on a WS row.

SHAPE SHOULDERS

Rows 1–2 Cast off 10 [11, 9, 11] sts, rib to end (84 [90, 100, 102] sts).

Rows 3–8 Cast off 7 [8, 7, 7] sts, rib to end (42 [42, 58, 60] sts).

Rows 9–10 SIZES 38 & 40 ONLY
Cast off 0 [0, 7, 7] sts, rib to end.
ALL SIZES
Cast off rem 42 [42, 44, 46] sts.

FRONT

Work as for Back until work measures 10¾ [11¼, 11¾, 12]in (27 [28, 29, 30]cm), ending on a WS row.

On next row, rib over 53 [57, 61, 65] sts, then p1, p2 tog, yrn, p1, yrn, p twice into the next st, p2, p3 tog, p twice into the next st, p2, yrn, p1, yrn, p2 tog, p1, sl rem sts on to a st-holder or spare needle.

Cont working on 72 [76, 80, 84] sts.

Next row K1, k2 tog, yf, k1, yf, k4, k3 tog, k4, yf, k1, yf, k2 tog, k1, rib to end.

Now work in rib and fancy stitch pattern (in this position) as follows:

Row 1 Rib 53 [57, 61, 65], p1, p2 tog, yrn, p1, yrn, p4, p3 tog, p4, yrn, p1, yrn, p2 tog, p1.

Row 2 K1, k2 tog, yf, k1, yf, k4, k3 tog, k4, yf, k1, yf, k2 tog, k1, rib 53 [57, 61, 65].

Rows 3–6 Rep Rows 1 and 2 twice.

Row 7 Rib 53 [57, 61, 65], p3, p2 tog, p4, yrn, p1, yrn, p4, p2 tog, p3.

Row 8 K3, k2 tog, k4, yf, k1, yf, k4, k2 tog, k3, rib 53 [57, 61, 65].

Rows 9–12 Rep Rows 7 and 8 twice.
Cont to work (in rib and fancy pattern) without shaping until work measures 12½ [13, 13, 13]in (31.5 [32.5, 32.5, 32.5]cm), ending on a WS row.

SHAPE ARMHOLE

Cast off 4 sts at beginning of next and following 2 alt rows (60 [64, 68, 72] sts), then dec 1 st at same side on next 5 [5, 3, 5] rows (55 [59, 65, 67] sts). Cont without shaping until 2¾in (7cm) of fancy pattern have been worked, ending on a WS row.

Next row (RS) Rib 13 [17, 21, 23], p1, p2 tog, yrn, p1, yrn, p twice into next st, p2, p3 tog, p twice into next st, p2, yrn, p1, yrn, p2 tog, p1, rib 6 [6, 8, 8], then finish row in the rest of the fancy pattern.
Cont with two bands of patt until armhole measures 4¾ [4¾, 5¼, 5½]in (12 [12, 13, 14]cm from beginning of shaping, ending on a WS row.

Next row (RS) Patt 32 [36, 38, 40] sts, cast off 23 [23, 27, 27] sts. Cont over rem 32 [36, 38, 40] sts until armhole edge measures 6½ [6½, 7, 7¼]in (16.5 [16.5, 17.5, 18]cm), ending on a WS row.

SHAPE SHOULDER

Row 1 Cast off 11 [12, 10, 12] sts (armhole edge), patt to end (21 [24, 28, 28) sts).

Row 2 Patt to end.

124

Rows 3–8 Cast off 7 [8, 7, 7] sts, patt to end (0 [0, 7, 7] sts).

Cast off rem 0 [0, 7, 7] sts.

Join yarn to front edge of opposite side and complete this side to match.

SLEEVES (MAKE 2)
Cast on 81 [85, 89, 93] sts.
Work rib as follows:

Row 1 K0 [1, 0, 1], P1 [2, 1, 2], (k2, p2) 7 [7, 8, 8] times, k2, p19, then work in k2, p2 rib to last 3 [1, 3, 1] sts, then k2 [1, 2, 1], p1 [0, 1, 0].

Row 2 Rib 31 [33, 35, 37], k19, rib 31 [33, 35, 37].

Cont without shaping in patt (with ribbing at each side and fancy pattern in the centre), until work measures 2in (5cm). On next and every following 4th row, inc 1 st at each end of the row to 103 [107, 111, 115] sts. Cont until work measures 6¾in (17cm) from beginning.

SHAPE SLEEVE CAP
Cast off 4 [4, 5, 6] sts at beginning of next 2 rows. Dec 1 st at each end of every 3rd row until 75 [95, 85, 87] sts rem. Dec 1 st every other row until 47 sts rem. At the beginning of each of next 2 rows cast off 14 sts. Work 1½in (4cm) without shaping on rem 19 sts. Cast off.

NECKBAND (MAKE 2)
Cast on 5 sts and work in St-st until work measures 2¾ [2¾, 3, 3]in (7 [7, 7.5, 7.5]cm). Cast off.

MAKING UP
Do not press. Sew the shoulders together. Stitch the cast-off edges of the upper part of the sleeves to the side edges of the centre part. Sew the tops of the sleeves into the armholes. Sew up the side and sleeve seams. Stitch the two rolled bands of St-st to the neck edge of the front. Darn in ends.

BUTTONS
Work 4 ch and join into a ring. Now work 3 ch, then 15 tr (dc) into the ring. Join by a sl st to the top of the 3 ch at the beginning, gather round the tops of the trs (dc), stuff with odd bits of wool, draw up and stitch. Make 11 more buttons in the same way. Stitch these to left edge of the front opening and work button loops on the opposite side to match.

HALF BLOUSE

126

Two blouses in one! This 1950s American pattern gives you an elegant one-shouldered evening blouse. Add the optional top half (with side buttoning) for something a little warmer and less revealing. The crochet 'popcorn' stitch around the edges adds a fun touch and the luxuriously soft silk/merino blend yarn used here gives it a slight sheen.

MATERIALS
Fyberspates Scrumptious 4-ply, 45% silk, 55% merino, 399yds (365m) per 100g skein, as follows:

4 x 100g in Natural

1 pair 3mm (US #2–3) needles

2.75mm (US #C/2) crochet hook

5 buttons

SIZING
TO FIT BUST SIZES
34in / 36in / 38in / 40in
(85cm / 90cm / 95cm / 100cm)

ACTUAL FINISHED MEASUREMENTS
Bust
33in / 35in / 37in / 39in
(82.5cm / 87.5cm / 92.5cm / 97.5cm)

Length (shoulder–hem)
18in / 19in / 19½in / 20¼in
(45cm / 48cm / 49cm / 51cm)

Length (hem–underarm)
11in / 11½in / 11½in / 12in
(27.5cm / 29cm / 29cm / 30cm)

Armhole depth
7in / 7½in / 8in / 8¼in
(17.5cm / 19cm / 20cm / 21cm)

Inner sleeve
3in / 3½in / 3½in / 3¾in
(7.5cm / 9cm / 9cm / 9.5cm)

TENSION
28 sts & 40 rows = 4in (10cm) over Stocking stitch.

ABBREVIATIONS
See page 11

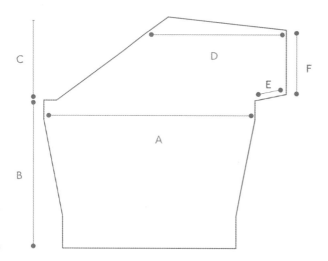

DIRECTIONS

BACK (MAKE 2)
Cast on 102 [108, 116, 122] sts. Work in
k1, p1 rib for 2½in (6.5cm). Cont in St-st,
inc 1 st at each edge on next and every
following 6 rows until 122 [130, 138, 146]
sts. Cont without shaping until work
measures 11 [11½, 11½, 12]in (27.5 [29, 29,
30]cm) from beginning, ending on a
WS row.

SHAPE SLEEVE AND NECK
Shape both edges AT THE SAME TIME
as follows:

Row 1   (RS) Cast off 7 [12, 14, 16] sts,
         k to end (115 [118, 124, 130] sts).

Row 2   Inc 1, p to last 2 sts, p2 tog
         (115 [118, 124, 130] sts).

Row 3   K2 tog, k to end (114 [117, 123, 129] sts).

Rows 4–17 Rep Rows 2 and 3 seven more times
         (107 [110, 116, 122] sts).

Row 18   Cast on 8 [9, 9, 10] sts, p to last
         2 sts, p2 tog (114 [118, 124, 131] sts).

Row 19   Rep Row 3 (113 [117, 123, 130] sts).

Row 20   Rep Row 18 (120 [125, 131, 130] sts).

Row 21   Rep Row 3 (119 [124, 130, 138] sts).

Row 22   P to last 2 sts, p2 tog.

         Rep Rows 21 and 22 (working straight
         at the sleeve edge and decreasing 1 st
         at the neck edge) until 72 [84, 75, 82]
         sts rem, ending on a RS row.

SHAPE SHOULDER
Row 1   Cast off 8 [9, 9, 10] sts, p to last
         2 sts, p2 tog.

Row 2   K2 tog, k to end.

Rows 3–12 Rep Rows 1 and 2 five times
         (12 [18, 9, 10] sts).
         Cast off rem sts.

A 16½ (17½, 18½, 19½)in
   41 (44, 46.5, 49)cm

B 11 (11½, 11½, 12)in
   27.5 (29, 29, 30)cm

C 7 (7½, 8, 8¼)in
   17.5 (19, 20, 21)cm

D 9½ (9¾, 10, 10¾)in
   24 (24.5, 25, 27)cm

E 3 (3½, 3½, 3¾)in
   7.5 (9, 9, 9.5)cm

F 5 (5½, 6, 6¼)in
   12.5 (14, 15, 15.5)cm

FRONT (MAKE 2)
Work as for Back, but reverse shaping.

MAKING UP
The crochet edgings are written in UK crochet terms with the US equivalent in brackets.

Press all pieces through a damp cloth on WS of work.

First Half
Sew shoulder, side and sleeve seams. Using 2.75mm crochet hook, work popcorn edging around neck and sleeve edges (see below).

Second Half
Sew shoulder seam. Sew side and sleeve seam but leave left side open (opposite sleeve). Work popcorn edging around neck and sleeve edges (see below).

Side Edging
Work 5 rows dc (sc) on back edge of side opening. On front edge of side opening, work 4 rows dc (sc). On the next row, make 5 button loops as follows: dc (sc) in first dc (sc), ch 3, skip 2 dc (sc) (button loop), dc (sc) in next dc (sc). Make 4 more button loops evenly spaced so that last button loop will be at end of row. Sew on buttons. Darn in ends.

Popcorn Edging
(necklines and sleeve edges)
With matching yarn and RS facing, attach yarn at underarm, dc (sc) in edge, *ch 1, skip ¼in (0.5cm) of edge, in next st make 4 tr (dc), drop loop from hook, insert hook under the ch 1 before the 4 tr (dc), pick up dropped loop and pull it through, ch 1 tightly (popcorn made), ch 1, skip ¼in (0.5cm) of edge, dc (sc) in next st; rep from * around, spacing popcorns about ½in (1.25cm) apart and ending with sl st in first dc (sc). Fasten off.

TWO-COLOUR SPOT JERSEY

This is a great 1940s jersey in a familiar vintage style. Its simple shape is decorated with classic details; the contrast yoke, stranded colourwork, small collar and high waist are instantly recognizable from that era. Add a couple of knitted shoulder pads as the original pattern suggested to give it a firmer, more boxy shape.

DIFFICULTY
++┼┼┼

MATERIALS

Jamieson's Spindrift 2-ply, 100% Shetland wool, 115yds (105m) per 25g ball, as follows:
6 [6, 6, 7] x 25g in Shade #123 (Oxford) (MC)

4 [5, 5, 5] x 25g in Shade #390 (Daffodil) (CC)

1 pair 3.25mm (US #3) needles

1 pair 2.75mm (US #2) needles

A set of 4 x 2.75mm (US #2) dpns

SIZING

TO FIT BUST SIZES
34in / 36in / 38in / 40in
(85cm / 90cm / 95cm / 100cm)

ACTUAL FINISHED MEASUREMENTS
Bust
35in / 37in / 39in / 41in
(88cm / 93cm / 98cm / 103cm)

Length (shoulder–hem)
19$\frac{1}{2}$in / 20in / 20$\frac{1}{2}$in / 21in
(49cm / 50.5cm / 51.5cm / 52.5cm)

Length (hem–underarm)
13in / 13$\frac{1}{2}$in / 13$\frac{1}{2}$in / 13$\frac{3}{4}$in
(32.5cm / 34cm / 34cm / 34.5cm)

Armhole depth
6$\frac{1}{2}$in / 6$\frac{1}{2}$in / 7in / 7$\frac{1}{4}$in
(16.5cm / 16.5cm / 17.5cm / 18cm)

Shoulder to shoulder
14$\frac{1}{2}$in / 15in / 15$\frac{1}{2}$in / 16in
(36.5cm / 37.5cm / 39cm / 40cm)

Inner sleeve
4$\frac{1}{2}$in / 4$\frac{1}{2}$in / 4$\frac{1}{2}$in / 4$\frac{1}{2}$in
(11.5cm / 11.5cm / 11.5cm / 11.5cm)

TENSION

30 sts & 36 rows = 4in (10cm) using 3.25mm needles over Stocking stitch colour pattern.

ABBREVIATIONS

See page 11

PATTERN & STITCH NOTES

Take care to weave in colour not in use loosely on WS of work in order to avoid a drawn, tight appearance and retain elasticity. See chart on page 139.

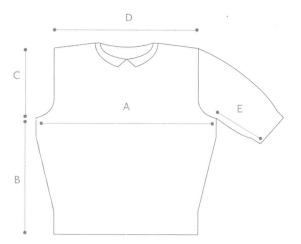

A 17½ (18½, 19½, 20½)in
   44 (46.5, 49, 51.5)cm

B 13 (13½, 13½, 13¾)in
   32.5 (34, 34, 34.5)cm

C 6½ (6½, 7, 7¼)in
   16.5 (16.5, 17.5, 18)cm

D 14½ (15, 15½, 16)in
   36.5 (37.5, 39, 40)cm

E 4½ (4½, 4½, 4½)in
   11.5 (11.5, 11.5, 11.5)cm

134

DIRECTIONS

FRONT

With 2.75mm needles and MC, cast on 113 [117, 121, 125] sts and work 3in (7.5cm) in k1, p1 rib.

Change to 3.25mm needles and work in spot patt as follows, AT THE SAME TIME inc 1 st at each end of every 6th row to 131 [137, 145, 153] sts, working these extra sts into the patt:

Row 1   K1 [3, 1, 3] MC, *k3 CC, k5 MC; rep from * to last 0 [2, 0, 2] sts, k0 [2, 0, 2] MC.

Row 2   P0 [2, 0, 2] MC, *p5 MC, p1 CC, p1 MC, p1 CC; rep from * to last 1 [3, 1, 3] sts, p to end in MC.

Row 3   Rep Row 1.

Row 4   P to end in MC.

Row 5   K to end in MC.

Row 6   Rep Row 4.

Row 7   Rep Row 5.

Row 8   P1 [3, 1, 3] MC, *p3 CC, p5 MC; rep from * to last 0 [2, 0, 2] sts, p0 [2, 0, 2] MC.

Row 9   K0 [2, 0, 2] MC, *k5 MC, k1 CC, k1 MC, k1 CC; rep from * to last 1 [3, 1, 3] sts, k to end in MC.

Row 10   Rep Row 8.

Row 11   K to end in MC.

Row 12   P to end in MC.

Row 13   Rep Row 7.

Row 14   Rep Row 12.
These 14 rows form one complete patt. Cont without shaping until work measures 13 [13½, 13½, 13¾]in (32.5 [34, 34, 34.5]cm).

SHAPE ARMHOLES

Keeping continuity of patt, cast off 6 [6, 7, 7] sts at beginning of next 2 rows (119 [125, 131, 139] sts).

Dec 1 st at each end of every following row until 109 [113, 117, 119] sts rem.

Cont without shaping until 8 [8, 9, 9] complete stitch pattern groups have been completed throughout the garment, ending on a 14th row. Work from cast-on edge should measure approx 15½ [15½, 17, 17]in (39 [39, 42.5, 42.5]cm).

YOKE

Cont in patt for yoke, reversing patt by using CC in place of MC, and MC in place of CC, until 1½ reps of the dark contrast yoke patt have been completed, ending on Row 7 (approx 2½in/6.25cm).

SHAPE NECK

Next row (RS) Patt across 44 [46, 48, 49] sts, turn. Cont in patt on these sts, AT THE SAME TIME dec 1 st at neck edge on every row until 34 [36, 38, 41] sts rem.

Cont without shaping until work measures 19½ [20, 20½, 21]in (49 [50.5, 51.5, 52.5]cm), ending at armhole edge.

SHAPE SHOULDERS

Row 1 Cast off 10 [9, 11, 11] sts, patt to end (24 [27, 27, 30] sts).

Row 2 Patt to end.

Row 3 Cast off 8 [9, 9, 10] sts, patt to end (16 [18, 18, 20] sts).

Rows 4–5 Rep Rows 2 and 3 once (8 [9, 9, 10] sts).

Row 6 Rep Row 2.
Cast off rem 8 [9, 9, 10] sts.

Return to main set of sts, sl centre 21 sts on to a spare needle and leave for collar, work on rem 44 [46, 47, 48] sts in patt to match first side.

BACK

Work exactly as given for Front, but cont straight (without neck shaping) in yoke patt until work measures 19½ [20, 20½, 21]in (49 [50.5, 51.5, 52.5]cm), ending on a WS row (109 [113, 117, 119] sts).

SHAPE NECK & SHOULDERS

Row 1 (RS) Cast off 10 [10, 11, 10] sts, patt until 30 [32, 33, 35] sts are on needle, turn.

Row 2 K2 tog, patt to end (29 [31, 32, 34] sts).

Row 3 Cast off 9 [9, 10, 10] sts, patt to last 2 sts, k2 tog (19 [21, 21, 23] sts).

Row 4 Rep Row 2 (18 [20, 20, 22] sts).

Row 5 Cast off 8 [9, 9, 10] sts, patt to last 2 sts, k2 tog (9 [10, 10, 11] sts).

Row 6 Rep Row 2 (8 [9, 9, 10] sts).
Cast off rem 8 [9, 9, 10] sts.

Return to main set of sts, sl centre 29 sts onto a st-holder, rejoin yarn to neck edge of rem 40 [42, 44, 45] sts and patt 1 row to armhole edge.

Work on rem sts in patt to match first side shapings.

SLEEVES (MAKE 2)

With 2.75mm needles and MC, cast on 80 [80, 82, 86] sts and work 1in (2.5cm) in k1, p1 rib, inc 1 st at end of last row (81 [81, 83, 87] sts).

Now cont in patt as given for front yoke (i.e. MC spots on CC background), inc 1 st at both ends of 5th row and every following 4th row to 85 [85, 87, 91] sts. (Work measures approx 2in/5cm.)

Change to 3.25mm needles and cont in patt, inc as before on every 4th row to 97 [97, 99, 103] sts.

Cont without shaping until work measures 5in (12.5cm), ending with WS.

SHAPE SLEEVE CAP

Keeping continuity of patt, dec 1 st at both ends of every other row until 81 sts rem, then dec on every row until 33 [33, 37, 39] sts rem. Cast off rem 33 [33, 37, 39] sts.

COLLAR

Sew shoulder seams. Sl 10 sts from centre front onto a 2.75mm needle then, starting at centre front with 2.75mm needles and MC, work across the rem 11 sts as follows:

Next row (K1, p1) 5 times, k1; k up 18 sts along neck edge to shoulder seam, with a second 2.75mm needle k up 6 sts down neck edge.

Work across 29 sts from st-holder as follows:
(P1, k1) 14 times, p1 then k up 6 sts up neck edge to shoulder seam, with a third needle k up 18 sts along neck edge, then work across 10 sts as follows: (k1, p1) 5 times.

Work in rounds of k1, p1 rib for ½in (1.5cm), ending at centre front, then work for collar as follows:

Next row Work in k1, p1 rib to end, turn.

Next row Work in k1, p1 rib to end.

Cont repeating last two rows, working in rows of k1, p1 rib for 1½in (4cm). Cast off loosely in rib.

MAKING UP

Press pieces lightly on WS using a warm iron over a damp cloth, taking care to avoid ribbed welts. Sew shoulder and side seams, taking care to match yoke contrasts. Sew sleeve seams and sew sleeves into armholes. Darn in ends.

Make 2 shoulder pads (see page 10) and secure to shoulders.

MAIN BODY

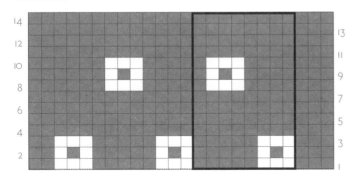

Key

■ MC (Oxford); k on RS, p on WS

□ CC (Daffodil); k on RS, p on WS

□ Pattern repeat

YOKE

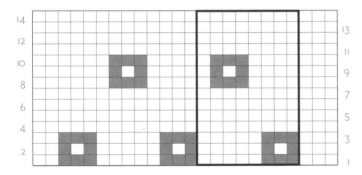

Key

■ MC (Oxford); k on RS, p on WS

□ CC (Daffodil); k on RS, p on WS

□ Pattern repeat

If you prefer working from a chart, use these charts. Work Row 1 of the colour pattern from the written instructions and then follow the chart.

A WAISTCOAT IN CLOQUE PATTERN

140

This short, neat waistcoat lends any outfit a smart tailored look. The textured 'cloque' stitch pattern combined with the wide contrast welts can be set off wonderfully by the style and colour of button you choose to finish with. It is made slightly looser than the average close-fitting vintage knit so it can be worn over a blouse or T-shirt.

DIFFICULTY
++┼┼┼

MATERIALS
Jamieson's Spindrift 2-ply, 100%
Shetland wool, 115yds (105m) per
25g ball, as follows:

5 [6] x 25g in Shade #435 (Apricot) (MC)

4 [4] x 25g in Shade #462 (Ginger) (CC)

1 pair 3.75mm (US #5) needles

1 pair 3mm (US #2–3) needles

3.75mm (US #F/5) crochet hook

13in (32.5cm) zip

10 buttons

SIZING
TO FIT BUST SIZES
34in / 36in / 38in / 40in
(85cm / 90cm / 95cm / 100cm)

ACTUAL FINISHED MEASUREMENTS
Bust
36in / 38in / 40in / 42in
(90cm / 95cm / 100cm / 105cm)

Length (shoulder–hem)
17½in / 17½in / 19in / 19in
(44cm / 44cm / 48cm / 48cm)

Length (hem–underarm)
10½in / 10½in / 11½in / 11½in
(26.5cm / 26.5cm / 29cm / 29cm)

Armhole depth
7in / 7in / 7½in / 7½in
(17.5cm / 17.5cm / 19cm / 19cm)

Shoulder to shoulder
14in / 14in / 15in / 15¾in
(35cm / 35cm / 37.5cm / 39.5cm)

TENSION
24 sts & 40 rows = 4in (10cm) using
3.75mm needles over unstretched
cloque stitch pattern.

To create your tension square, cast
on 24 sts, follow the stitch pattern
below and rep from * to * twice.
For the tension square purposes,
the stitch pattern includes 4 extra
stitches (2 either side of the patt reps).

ABBREVIATIONS
See page 11

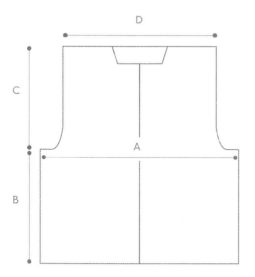

STITCH PATTERN

The st patt is worked over 10 sts and 20 rows — the number of reps will depend on your chosen size. Check how to work the patt according to your size. The written instructions for each rep are as follows:

Row 1	K.
Row 2	P.
Row 3	K.
Row 4	P2, *k twice into each of next 2 sts, p8; rep from * to last 2 sts, p2.
Row 5	K2, *k8, p4, k8; rep from * to last 2 sts, k2.
Row 6	P2, *k4, p8; rep from * to last 2 sts, p2.
Rows 7–9	Rep Rows 5 and 6 once more, then Row 5 once.
Row 10	P2, *(k2 tog) twice, p8; rep from * to last 2 sts, p2.
Rows 11–13	Rep Rows 1–3.
Row 14	P2, *p6, k twice into each of next 2 sts, p2; rep from * to last 2 sts, p2.
Row 15	K2, *k2, p4, k6; rep from * to last 2 sts, k2.
Row 16	P2, *p6, k4, p2; rep from * to last 2 sts, p2.
Rows 17–19	Rep Rows 15 and 16 once, then Row 15 once.
Row 20	P2, *p6,(k2 tog) twice, p2*, p2.

Please note that the 'cloque' pattern increases the st count by 2 sts on Rows 4 and 14, and reduces it again on Rows 10 and 20 once the pattern rep is completed. This means that when shaping is made at the armhole edges, care must be taken not to decrease into an 'open' patt rep or a false st count will be reached. If in doubt, work one patt rep less at the edges. Similarly, when the final cast-off is made at the shoulders, take care to 'close' the cloque patt before casting off.

A   18 (19, 20, 21)in
    45 (47.5, 50, 52.5)cm

B   10½ (10½, 11½, 11½)in
    26.5 (26.5, 29, 29)cm

C   7 (7, 7½, 7½)in
    17.5 (17.5, 19, 19)cm

D   14 (14, 15, 15¾)in
    35 (35, 37.5, 39.5)cm

DIRECTIONS

BACK

With 3mm needles and CC, cast on 110 [114, 122, 126] sts and work in k1, p1 rib for 3in (7.5cm).

Change to 3.75mm needles and MC. Work in patt as follows:

Row 1   (RS) K.

Row 2   K.

Row 3   P.

Row 4   K.

Row 5   P4 [1, 5, 2], *k twice into each of next 2 sts, p8; rep from * 9 [10, 10, 11] times more to last 6 [3, 7, 4] sts, k twice into each of next 2 sts, p to end of row.

Row 6   K4 [1, 5, 2], *p4, k8; rep from * 9 [10, 10, 11] times more to last 8 [5, 9, 6] sts, p4, k to end of row.

Row 7   P4 [1, 5, 2], *k4, p8; rep from * 9 [10, 10, 11] times more to last 8 [5, 9, 6] sts, k4, p to end of row.

Rows 8–10   Rep Rows 6 and 7 once more, then Row 6 once.

Row 11   P4 [1, 5, 2], *(k2 tog) twice, p8; rep from * 9 [10, 10, 11] times more to last 8 [5, 9, 6] sts, (k2 tog) twice, p to end of row.

Rows 12–14   Rep Rows 2–4.

Row 15   P9 [6, 10, 7], *k twice into each of next 2 sts, p8; rep from * 8 [9, 9, 10] times more to last 11 [8, 12, 9] sts, k twice into each of next 2 sts, p to end of row.

Row 16   K9 [6, 10, 7], *p4, k8; rep from * 8 [9, 9, 10] times more to last 13 [10, 14, 11] sts, p4, k to end of row.

Row 17   P9 [6, 10, 7], *k4, p8; rep from * 8 [9, 9, 10] times more to last 13 [10, 14, 11] sts, k4, p to end of row.

Rows 18–20   Rep Rows 16 and 17 once, then Row 16 once.

Row 21   P9 [6, 10, 7], *(k2 tog) twice, p8; rep from * 8 [9, 9, 10] times more until last 13 [10, 14, 11] sts, (k2 tog) twice, p to end of row.

Rep Rows 2–21 until work measures approx 10½ [10½, 11½, 11½]in (26.5 [26.5, 29, 29]cm) or desired length from cast-on edge, ending on a Row 2 or Row 12 (WS) (110 [114, 122, 126] sts).

SHAPE ARMHOLES

With RS facing, cast off 8 [8, 9, 9] sts from beginning of next 2 rows (94 [98, 104, 108] sts).

Keeping in patt, k2 tog at each end of next and every other row until 84 [84, 90, 94] sts rem.

Cont in patt without further shaping until the armhole measures 7 [7, 7½, 7½]in (17.5 [17.5, 19, 19]cm) from beginning of shaping, ending on a WS row. Cast off.

RIGHT FRONT

With 3mm needles and CC, cast on 54 [56, 60, 62] sts. and knit in k1, p1 rib for 3in (7.5cm).

Change to 3.75mm needles and MC. Work in patt as follows:

Row 1   (RS) K.

Row 2   K.

Row 3   P.

Row 4   K.

Row 5   P1 [2, 4, 5] sts, *k twice into each of next 2 sts, p8; rep from * 4 [4, 4, 4] times more until last 3 [4, 6, 7] sts, k twice into each of next 2 sts, p to end of row.

Row 6   K1 [2, 4, 5] sts, *p4, k8; rep from * 4 [4, 4, 4] times more until last 5 [6, 8, 9] sts, p4, k to end of row.

Row 7	P1 [2, 4, 5] sts, *k4, p8; rep from * 4 [4, 4, 4] times more until last 5 [6, 8, 9] sts, k4, p to end of row.
Rows 8–10	Rep Rows 6 and 7 once more, then Row 6 once.
Row 11	P2 [3, 5, 1] sts, *(k2 tog) twice, p8; rep from * 4 [4, 4, 4] times more until last 2 [3, 5, 1] sts, p to end of row.
Rows 12–14	Rep Rows 2–4.
Row 15	P4 [5, 7, 8] sts, *p2, k twice into each of next 2 sts, p6; rep from * 3 [3, 3, 3] times more until last 0 [1, 3, 4] sts, p to end of row.
Row 16	K0 [1, 3, 4] sts, *k6, p4, k2; rep from * 3 [3, 3, 3] times more until last 4 [5, 7, 8] sts, k to end of row.
Row 17	P4 [5, 7, 8] sts, *p2, k4, p6; rep from * 3 [3, 3, 3] times more until last 0 [1, 3, 4] sts, p to end of row.
Rows 18–20	Rep Rows 16 and 17 once, then Row 16 once.
Row 21	P4 [5, 7, 8] sts, *p2, (k2 tog) twice, p6; rep from * 3 [3, 3, 3] times more until last 0 [1, 3, 4] sts, p to end of row.

Rep Rows 2–21 until work measures the same as Back to armhole (10½ [10½, 11½, 11½]in/26.5 [26.5, 29, 29]cm), ending on a Row 3 or a Row 13.

SHAPE ARMHOLES

With WS of work facing, cast off 8 [8, 9, 9] sts (46 [48, 51, 53] sts).

Dec 1 st at beginning of next alt and every other row (armhole edge) until 41 [41, 43, 45] sts rem.

Cont in patt without further shaping until armhole measures 5 [5, 5½, 5½]in (12.5 [12.5, 14, 14]cm) from beginning of shaping, ending on a WS row.

NECK SHAPING

With RS facing, dec 1 st, patt to end (40 [40, 42, 44] sts).

Next row	Patt to end.
Next row	Rep last 2 rows 7 times more. (33 [33, 35, 37] sts). Cast off rem sts.

LEFT FRONT

Work as for Right Front, working armhole and neck shapings on opposite ends of rows.

FRONT BANDS

With 3mm needles and CC, cast on 32 sts and work in k1, p1 rib for 13in (32.5cm).

Cast off 2 sts at beginning of every other row 7 times (18 sts). Cast off ribwise.

Make a second band like this, but cast off on opposite side of work.

MAKING UP

Press pieces lightly on WS using a warm iron over a damp cloth, taking care to avoid ribbed welts. Sew the front bands with the long sides to the front edges of the bodice, starting at the bottom and working up to the neck. Make sure that both bands end exactly opposite each other at the top. Join the side and shoulder seams.

Divide armhole edges into three sections. With 3mm dpns and CC, pick up and k 114 [114, 120, 120] sts around the armhole, spreading the sts evenly over three needles — there should be 38 [38, 40, 40] sts on each needle. Work in k1, p1 rib for 1in (2.5cm). Cast off in rib.

Fold front CC bands over for a little more than half their width, and secure with five buttons. Insert the zip down the centre front, fitting flush with the top opening but leaving a gap at the bottom (see photographs).

With MC and 3.75mm crochet hook, work 1 row of dc (sc) around back neck and neck sides. Darn in ends.

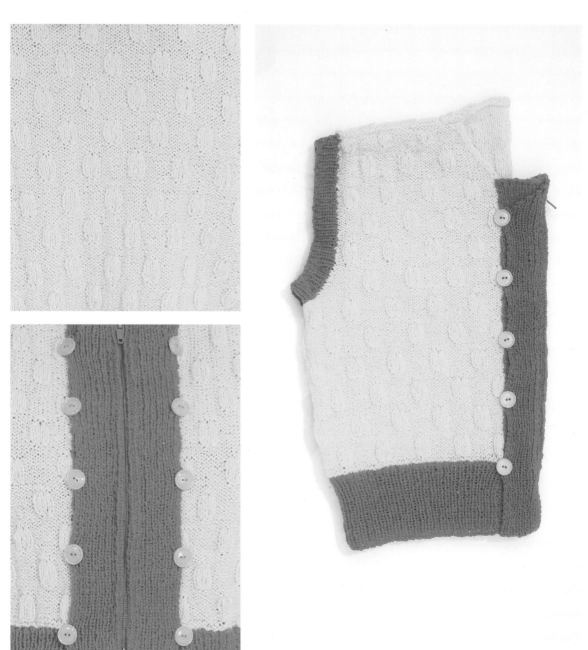

CHARMING DRESS

This beautiful 1930s dress is worked in
a delicate yet firm textured stitch, with
contrasting bands of moss stitch at the
yoke and belt. Mainly knitted in the round,
the skirt is divided into panels and shaped
to give it some flare, tapering up to a ribbed
waistline. Finished with knitted buttons to
match the belt, this is a real head-turner.

DIFFICULTY
+++++

MATERIALS

Holst Garn Supersoft 2-ply, 100% wool,
627yds (575m) per 100g ball, as follows:

11 x 50g in Shade #CO34 (Dark Navy) (A)

1 x 50g in Shade #068 (Peony) (B)

1 x 50g in Shade #045 (Sapphire) (C)

1 3.75mm (US #5) circular needle
(40in/100cm)

1 3.75mm (US #5) circular needle
(32in/80cm)

1 pair 3.75mm (US #5) needles

1 pair 3mm (US #2–3) needles

1 set of 4 x 2mm (US #0) dpns

2.5mm (US #B/1–C/2) crochet hook

6 x ¾in (22mm) button moulds for
yoke and belt (or yarn ends to stuff)

SIZING

TO FIT BUST SIZES
34in / 36in / 38in / 40in
(85cm / 90cm / 95cm / 100cm)

ACTUAL FINISHED MEASUREMENTS
Bust
33in / 35in / 37in / 39in
(83cm / 88cm / 93cm / 98cm)

Waist (over stretchy rib)
25in / 27in / 29¼in / 31¾in
(62.5cm / 67.5cm / 73cm / 79.3cm)

Length (shoulder–hem)
41½in / 42½in / 44¼in / 46in
103.5cm / 106.5cm / 110.5cm / 115.5cm

Length (shoulder–waist)
15½in / 16½in / 17¼in / 18in
(38.5cm / 41.5cm / 43cm / 45.5cm)

Length (waist–underarm)
9in / 9½in / 10in / 10½in
(22.5cm / 24cm / 25cm / 26.5cm)

Skirt length (waist–hem)
26in / 26in / 27in / 28in
(65cm / 65cm / 67.5cm / 70cm)

Armhole depth
6½in / 7in / 7¼in / 7½in
(16cm / 17.5cm / 18cm / 19cm)

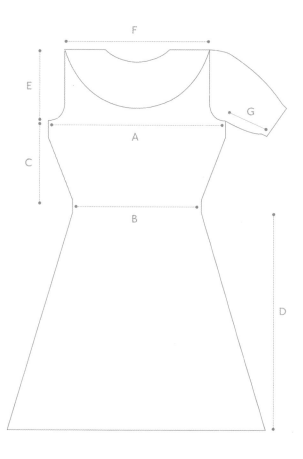

Shoulder to shoulder
14in / 14in / 14½in / 14½in
(35cm / 35cm / 36.5cm / 36.5cm)

Inner sleeve
4½in / 4½in / 4½in / 4½in
(11.5cm / 11.5cm / 11.5cm / 11.5cm)

TENSION
30 sts & 34 rows = 4in (10cm) using
3.75mm needles over unstretched
main stitch pattern.

30 sts & 40 rows = 4in (10cm) using
3.75mm needles over moss stitch.

36 sts & 44 rows = 4in (10cm) using
3mm needles over moss stitch.

40 sts & 52 rows = 4in (10cm) using
2mm needles over moss stitch.

PATTERN & STITCH NOTES
When casting on in the round, make
absolutely sure not to twist the sts —
this is easily done when you have so
many sts on your needle. The main
part of the dress is worked in the round
using a sl-st patt on RS as follows:

Rnd 1   *K1, sl 1 knitwise; rep from * to end.

Rnd 2   K.

Rnd 3   *Sl 1 knitwise, k1; rep from * to end.

Rnd 4   K.

The skirt is divided into panels by
working 2 p sts. These panels are
decreased as the fabric is worked to
create a slightly flared skirt. Since you
are knitting in the round, you will always
be working on the RS of the fabric.

The sleeves and upper part of the dress
(from armhole shapings onwards) are
worked in the same st but worked back
and forth, using 2 needles instead of
circulars. This is worked as follows:

Row 1   (RS) *K1, sl 1 knitwise; rep from * to end.

Row 2   P.

Row 3   *Sl 1 knitwise, k1; rep from * to end.

Rnd 4   P.

A   16½ (17½, 18½, 19½)in
    41.5 (44, 46.5, 49)cm

B   12½ (13½, 14½, 15¾)in
    31 (33.5, 36.5, 39.5)cm

C   9 (9½, 10, 10½)in
    22.5 (24, 25, 26.5)cm

D   26 (26, 27, 28)in
    65 (65, 67.5, 70)cm

E   6½ (7, 7¼, 7½)in
    16 (17.5, 18, 19)cm

F   14 (14, 14½, 14½)in
    35 (35, 36.5, 36.5)cm

G   4½ (4½, 4½, 4½)in
    11.5 (11.5, 11.5, 11.5)cm

The yoke is worked in 3 different coloured stripes of moss-st, decreasing at regular intervals and changing to smaller needles to create the circular shape.

ABBREVIATIONS
See page 11

DIRECTIONS

With A and a 3.75mm circular needle 100cm long, cast on 450 [470, 490, 510] sts.

Rnd 1 *(K1, sl 1 knitwise) 21 [22, 23, 24] times, k1, p2 (creates narrow rib to separate panel); rep from * to end of rnd.

Rnd 2 *K43 [45, 47, 49], p2; rep from * to end of rnd.

Rnd 3 *(Sl 1 knitwise, k1) 21 [22, 23, 24] times, sl 1 knitwise, p2; rep from * to end of rnd.

Rnd 4 *K43 [45, 47, 49], p2; rep from * to end of rnd.

These 4 rnds comprise one patt. Cont to rep them until the piece measures 2in (2.5cm) from start, ending with Rnd 1. Now begin the shaping as follows:

Dec rnd 1 (A Rnd 2 patt) *K2 tog, k41 [43, 45, 47], p2; rep from * to end of rnd (440 [460, 480, 500] sts).

Next rnd *(K1, sl 1 knitwise) 21 [22, 23, 24] times, p2; rep from * to end of rnd.

Next rnd *K42 [44, 46, 48], p2; rep from * to end of rnd.

Next rnd (A Rnd 1 patt): *(Sl 1 knitwise, k1) 21 [22, 23, 24] times, p2; rep from * to end of rnd.

Next rnd *K42 [44, 46, 48], p2; rep from * to end of rnd.
Rep the last 4 rnds once more, then rep the first 3 again.

Dec rnd 2 (A Rnd 2 patt): *K40 [42, 44, 46], k2 tog, p2; rep from * to end of rnd (430 [450, 470, 490] sts.

Next rnd *(K1, sl 1 knitwise) 20 [21, 22, 23] times, k1, p2; rep from * to end of rnd.

Next rnd *K41 [43, 45, 47], p2; rep from * to end of rnd.

Next rnd (A Rnd 1 patt): *(Sl 1 knitwise, k1) 20 [21, 22, 23] times, sl 1 knitwise, p2; rep from * to end of rnd.

Next rnd *K41 [43, 45, 47], p2; rep from * to end of rnd.

Rep the last 4 rnds once more, then the first 3 of them again.

Dec rnd 3 (A Rnd 2 patt): *K2 tog, k39 [41, 43, 45], p2; rep from * to end of rnd (420 [440, 460, 480] sts).

Keeping continuity of patt, cont in this way, dec 1 st at alt edges of each panel in every 12th rnd until you have worked Dec Rnd 24 and 210 [230, 250, 270] sts rem. Proceed without further dec until work measures approx 26 [26, 27, 28] in (65 [65, 67.5, 70]cm) from cast-on edge, ending with a Rnd 4, but when working last rnd, leave last st unworked and sl it onto the start of next rnd, so that the rnd now begins and ends with a p1.

Change to set of four 2mm dpns and work in rnds of k1, p1 rib for ½in (1.5cm), taking care to finish at completion of a rnd. With 3.75mm (80cm) long circular needle, proceed in patt for bodice as follows:

Bodice rnd 1 *Sl 1 knitwise, p1; rep from * to end.

Bodice rnd 2 K.

Bodice rnd 3 *P1, sl 1 knitwise; rep from * to end.

Bodice rnd 4 K.
Rep these 4 rnds once more, then work first 3 rnds again. Now begin to inc.

Inc rnd 1	K twice into first st, k103 [113, 123, 133], k twice into each of next 2 sts, k103 [113, 123, 133], k twice into last st (214 [234, 254, 274] sts).
	Keeping continuity of patt, work 11 rnds on these sts.
Inc rnd 2	K twice into the first st, k105 [115, 125, 135] sts, k twice into each of next 2 sts, k105 [115, 125, 135], k twice into last st.
	Cont to inc 4 sts in this way on every 12th rnd until there are 246 [262, 278, 292] sts on the needle. Cont without shaping until the work measures approx 9 [9½, 10, 10½]in (22.5 [24, 25, 26.5]cm) from waist ribbing (or desired length from waist to armhole), ending with a k rnd.

SHAPE ARMHOLES

Next rnd	Cast off 6 sts, then work in patt until you have worked 111 [119, 127, 134] sts after the first cast-off. Cast off the next 12 sts, then work in patt to end. Change to 3.75mm needles and work in rows instead of rnds, noting that every 2nd and 4th patt row will now be worked all p on WS instead of k on RS (see stitch pattern notes above). Leaving the first set of 111 [119, 127, 134] sts on a st-holder, proceed only on the second set of sts as follows:
Row 1	(WS) Cast off 6 sts and p to end (111 [119, 127, 134] sts).
**Row 2	K2 tog, then work in patt to end (110 [118, 126, 133] sts).
Row 3	P2 tog, then p to end (109 [117, 125, 132] sts).
	Rep last 2 rows until 103 [109, 115, 121] sts rem, then work without dec until the armhole is 1½ [1¾, 1¾, 1¾]in (3.5 [4.5, 4.5, 4.5]cm) deep, measured on the straight from 1st armhole row, and ending with a WS (p) row.

SHAPE YOKE LINE

Row 1	Work 40 [42, 44, 46] sts, cast off 23 [25, 27, 29] sts, work to end. Leaving the first set of 40 [42, 44, 46] sts on

a st-holder, cont on second set of 40 [42, 44, 46] sts as follows:

Next row	P.
Next row	Cast off 3 sts, work in patt to end (37 [39, 41, 43] sts).
Next row	P.
Next row	Cast off 2 sts, work in patt to end (35 [37, 39, 41] sts).
Next row	P. Cont in patt, dec 1 st at neck (inner) end of every row until all sts are worked off. Fasten off.
	Join yarn to inner end of other set of 40 [42, 44, 46] sts.
Next row	Cast off 3 sts, p to end (37 [39, 41, 43] sts).
Next row	Work in patt.
Next row	Cast off 2 sts, p to end (35 [37, 39, 41]. Work 1 row straight, then dec 1 st at neck end of every row until all sts are worked off. Fasten off.**

With WS of work facing, join yarn to end of other set of 111 [119, 127, 134] sts, and p1 row on WS. Now work as given for first side of bodice from ** to **.

SLEEVES (MAKE 2)

With 2mm needles and A, cast on 90 [94, 96, 98] sts and work in rows of k1, p1 rib for 1½in (3.5cm). Change to 3.75mm needles.

Patt row 1	(RS) *Sl 1 knitwise, p1; rep from * to end.
Patt row 2	P.
Patt row 3	*P1, sl 1 knitwise; rep from * to end.
Patt row 4	P.
	Rep these 4 rows until Sleeve measures 4½in (11.5cm), ending with a p row.

153

SHAPE SLEEVE CAP
Cast off 6 sts at beginning of each of next 2 rows (78 [82, 84, 86] sts), then dec I st at beginning of every row until 68 [72, 74, 76] sts rem.

Work 3in (7.5cm) on these sts without shaping, then dec I st at beginning of every row until 50 [54, 56, 58] sts rem. Cast off 5 sts at beginning of each of next 4 rows (30 [34, 36, 38] sts). Cast off.

YOKE
With 3.75mm needles and B, cast on 301 [321, 337, 353] sts and work in moss-st as follows:

Every row	KI, *pI, kI; rep from * to end.

Work IIn (2.5cm) in moss-st, then begin the decs and make buttonholes as follows:

Dec row I	Moss-st 4, cast off next 4 sts for a buttonhole, work I [3, 4, 3] sts so that you have 2 [4, 5, 4] sts on right-hand needle after cast-off; *k2 tog, p2 tog, moss-st IO; rep from * to last II [15, 16, 19] sts, k2 tog, p2 tog, moss-st to end (259 [277, 291, 305] sts).
Next row	Work in moss-st, but cast on 4 sts over those cast off in preceding row to complete the buttonhole.

Work ½in (1.5cm) in moss-st, ending at buttonhole edge, then change to 3mm needles and A, and work another ¼in (0.5cm) ending at buttonhole edge.

Dec row 2	Moss-st IO [12, 13, 12], *k2 tog, p2 tog, moss-st IO; rep from * to last II [13, 12, 13] sts, k2 tog, p2 tog, moss-st to end (223 [239, 251, 263] sts).

Cont on these sts until work measures 2½in (6.5cm) from start, ending at buttonhole edge. Make another buttonhole on the next 2 rows.

Dec row 3	Moss-st IO [12, 13, 12], *k2 tog, p2 tog, moss-st 6; rep from * to last 3 [7, 8, II] sts, moss-st 3 to end (181 [195, 205, 215] sts).

Cont in moss-st until work measures 3¼ [3¼, 3½, 3½]in (8 [8, 9, 9]cm) from start, ending at buttonhole edge, then change to 2mm needles and C, and work another ½in (1.5cm) in moss-st, finishing at buttonhole edge.

Dec row 4	Moss-st IO [12, 13, 12], *k2 tog, p2 tog, moss-st 4; rep from * to last 3 [7, 8, II] sts, moss-st to end (139 [151, 159, 167] sts).

Work I row on these sts, then make the third buttonhole on next 2 rows. Work 4 rows after the 3rd buttonhole.

Dec row 5	Moss-st IO [12, 13, 12], *k2 tog, p2 tog, moss-st 6; rep from * to last 9 [9, 6, 5] sts, k2 tog, p2 tog, moss-st to end (113 [123, 129, 135] sts).

Work I more row. Cast off.

BELT
With 3.75mm needles and B, cast on 195 [209, 223, 237] sts and work ½in (1.5cm) in moss-st. Now make a buttonhole as follows:

B'hole row I	Moss-st 4, cast off 4, moss-st to end.
B'hole row 2	Work in moss-st, cast on 4 sts over those cast off in previous row.

Work another ½in (1.5cm) in moss-st, finishing at buttonhole end. Break off B and join A. K I row.

Work ½in (1.5cm) in moss-st, finishing at buttonhole end, then make another buttonhole as before. Work another ½in (1.5cm) in moss-st, finishing at buttonhole end. Break off A, join C. K I row. Now rep from * to * once more. Cast off.

BUTTONS
The crochet buttons are written in UK crochet terms with the US equivalent in brackets.

Make 2 buttons in A, 2 in B and 2 in C for the belt and yoke.

With 2.5mm hook, work 4 ch and join into a ring with a sl st.

Rnd 1 Work 7 dc (sc) into ring.

Rnd 2 *Work 1 dc (sc) into first dc (sc), 2 dc (sc) into next dc (sc); rep from * twice more; 1 dc (sc) into last dc (sc).

Rnd 3 Work 1 dc (sc) into each dc (sc) of previous rnd.

Rep last rnd twice more, then place button mould into circle, break off yarn leaving an end, thread end in a needle, run it around edge of circle, draw up and fasten off.

MAKING UP
Press all pieces lightly on WS widthways (i.e. with the iron moving across the skirt from left to right rather than top to bottom) using a warm iron over a damp cloth.

Work 1 row of dc (sc) around curved top edge of bodice front and back.

Sew up sleeve seams, then sew sleeves into armholes, leaving the top of each sleeve free for joining to yoke.

Sew two dart-like pleats into top of each sleeve, placing each dart 1¼ [1¼, 1½, 1¾]in (3 [3, 4, 4.5]cm) from centre of sleeve top edge and ensuring that the folded dart fabric is facing outwards. The sleeve cast-off edge should now measure 2½ [3, 3¼, 3½]in (6 [7.5, 8, 9]cm).

Place the buttonhole edge of the yoke over the opposite edge and sew on buttons; then, with the buttons done up, match the centre front of the yoke to the centre front of the dress and place pins as markers. Sew yoke to top of bodice and sleeves, making the yoke's centre front and back match the central points of the dress. Work 1 row of dc (sc) around lower edge of skirt. Darn in ends.

Make 2 shoulder pads (see page 10) and secure to shoulders.

FASHIONABLE HOUSECOAT (IN FIVE COLOURS)

This early 1940s striped housecoat becomes a stunning full-length coat or cardigan. It is surprisingly simple and economical to knit on long needles in vintage knitter's favourite Jamieson & Smith 2-ply Jumper Yarn, and looks equally good if you use the reverse side as the right side. You can also work it in just two colours (see Pattern & Stitch Notes).

DIFFICULTY
++++

MATERIALS

Jamieson & Smith 2-ply Jumper Yarn, 100% pure new wool, 125yds (115m) per 25g ball, as follows:

11 x 25g in Shade #02 (Grey) (A)

5 x 25g in Shade #036 (Navy) (B)

6 x 25g in Shade #125 (Orange) (C)

6 x 25g in Shade #FC17 (Beige) (D)

6 x 25g in Shade #043 (Pink) (E)

1 pair 4.5mm (US #7) long needles

2.5mm (US B/1–C/2) crochet hook

2 large press studs, or hooks and eyes

1¹/₂yds (1.3m) x 1in (2.5cm) wide Petersham ribbon (stiff ribbon) for the waist

Length of ribbon for the belt

SIZING

TO FIT BUST (ONE SIZE)
34–40in (85–100cm)

ACTUAL FINISHED MEASUREMENTS
Bust
38in (95cm)

Waist
39in (97.5cm)

Length (shoulder–hem)
55in (137.5cm)

Length (waist–hem)
38in (95cm)

Length (waist–underarm)
10in (25cm)

Armhole depth
7in (17.5cm)

Shoulder to shoulder
16in (40cm)

Inner sleeve (inc cuff)
19in (47.5cm)

TENSION

24 sts & 28 rows = 4in (10cm) over Stocking stitch.

ABBREVIATIONS

See page 11

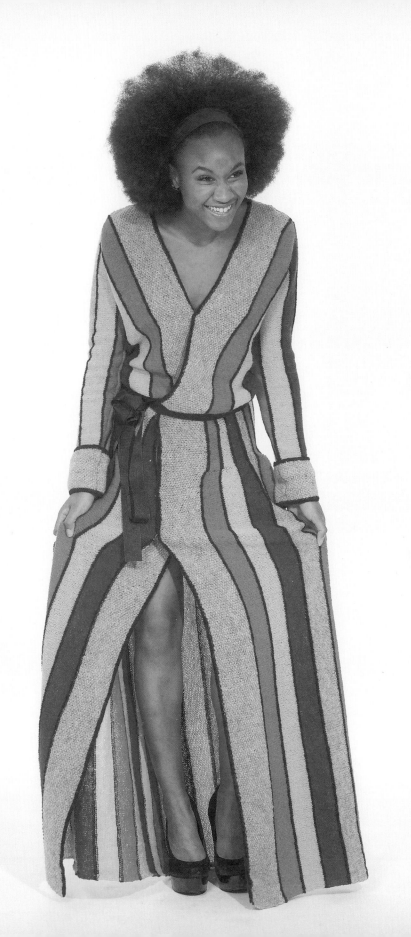

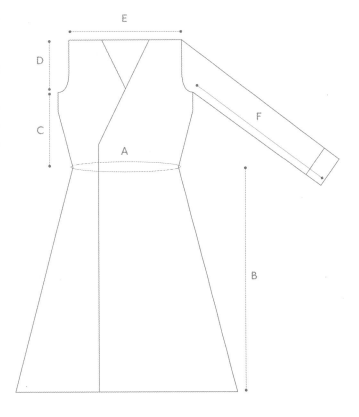

PATTERN & STITCH NOTES

The main part of the dress is worked in 14 rows of St-st stripes with 2 rows of darker garter-st 'dividers' as follows:

14 rows St-st in Grey (A)
2 rows garter-st (making 1 ridge) in Navy (B)
14 rows St-st in Orange (C)
2 rows garter-st in Navy (B)
14 rows St-st in Beige (D)
2 rows garter-st in Navy (B)
14 rows St-st in Pink (E)
2 rows garter-st in Navy (B)

These rows are repeated throughout the garment unless otherwise stated. The cuffs and borders are worked in moss-st. The skirt and bodice are knitted separately from side to side and the bodice fronts are knitted 'on the bias'. Shaping at the skirt's waist is made using short rows, and the garment is given a firmer structure by a band of ribbon sewn into the waist. You can work a shorter or longer skirt length by casting on fewer or more sts and continuing per the pattern — bear in mind that the weight of the fabric will stretch the garment a little, so if in doubt err on the side of a shorter length.

Please note that cast-off edges are usually tighter than cast-on edges — as the bodice and skirt are knitted side to side, take extra care not to cast off too tightly.

The stripe scheme could be altered by following an alternative route suggested in the original pattern: knit the coat in two colours with dark cuffs and dark borders (the borders knitted in 2 rows of garter-st, 4in (10cm) of moss-st and 2 rows of garter-st). The main part of the garment is then knitted in 14 rows of St-st in light, and 2 rows garter-st in dark throughout.

A	39in (max) (97.5cm)	D	7in (17.5cm)
B	38in (95cm)	E	16in (40cm)
C	10in (25cm)	F	19in (47.5cm)

DIRECTIONS

SKIRT

With B, cast on 229 sts and work 2 rows in garter-st.Change to A and work 4in (10cm) in moss-st as follows:

Row 1 K1, *p1, k1; rep from * to end.
Rep this row for 4in (10cm).

Change to B and work 2 rows in garter-st.

Change to C and cont in patt, working waist shaping as follows:

Row 1 (RS) Work to last 30 sts, w&t.

Row 2 Work to end.

Row 3 Work to end (remember to combine wrapped st).

Row 4 Work to end.
Cont in patt, rep last 4 rows in the st patt (see above) until lower edge of work measures approx 71in (177.5cm) finishing after a pink (E) stripe.

Change to B and work 2 rows in garter-st.

Change to A and work 4in (10cm) in moss-st.

Change to B and work 2 rows in garter-st.

With B, cast off, taking care to match the tension of cast-on edge.

BODICE BACK
SHAPE ARMHOLE AND WAIST

With A, cast on 16 sts and, starting at side edge, work in St-st as follows:

Row 1 (RS) K to end.

Row 2 Cast on 8 sts, p to end (24 sts).

Rows 3–6 Rep Rows 1 and 2 twice more (40 sts).

Row 7 K twice into first st, k to end (41 sts).

Row 8 Cast on 8 sts, p to last st, p twice into last st (50 sts).

Rows 9–10 Rep Rows 7 and 8 once (60 sts).

Row 11 K twice into first st, k to end (61 sts).

Row 12 P to last st, p twice into last st (62 sts).

Rows 13–14 Rep Rows 11 and 12 once (64 sts).
Change to B.

Row 15 Rep Row 11 (65 sts).

Row 16 K to last st, k twice into last st.
Cast on 30 sts (96 sts).

SHAPE RIGHT SHOULDER

Change to C and work 14 rows in St-st, inc 1 st at beginning of 11th row (a k row) (97 sts).

Change to B and work 2 rows in garter-st.

Change to D and work 14 rows in St-st, inc 1 st at beginning of 7th row (98 sts).

Change to B and work 2 rows in garter-st, inc 1 st at beginning of first row (99 sts).

Change to E and work 14 rows in St-st.

Change to B and work 2 rows in garter-st.

Change to A and work 14 rows in St-st.

Change to B and work 2 rows in garter-st.

Change to E and work 14 rows in St-st.

SHAPE LEFT SHOULDER

Change to B and work 2 rows in garter-st, dec 1 st at end of second row (at the shaped edge) (98 sts).

Change to D and work 14 rows in St-st, dec 1 st at beginning of 11th row (97 sts).

Change to B and work 2 rows in garter-st.

Change to C and work 14 rows in St-st, dec 1 st at beginning of 5th row (96 sts).

SHAPE ARMHOLE AND WAIST
Change to B.

Row 1 (RS) Cast off 31 sts, k to end (65 sts).

Row 2 K to last 2 sts, k2 tog (64 sts).

Change to A.

Row 3 K2 tog, k to end (63 sts).

162

Row 4	P to last 2 sts, p2 tog (62 sts).
Rows 5–6	Rep Rows 3 and 4 once (60 sts).
Row 7	K2 tog, k to end (59 sts).
Row 8	Cast off 8 sts, p to last 2 sts, p2 tog (50 sts).
Rows 9–10	Rep Rows 7 and 8 once (40 sts).
Row 11	K to end.
Row 12	Cast off 8 sts, p to end (32 sts).
Rows 13–16	Rep Rows 11 and 12 twice.
	Cast off rem 16 sts.

RIGHT FRONT
With B, cast on 128 sts and work 2 rows in garter-st.

Change to A and work 4in (10cm) in moss-st, dec 1 st at beginning of second row and at the same edge on every following 4th row (121 sts).

Change to B and work 2 rows in garter-st.

SHAPE ARMHOLE
Change to C and cont in patt, shaping as follows:

Row 1	K2 tog, k to last 2 sts, k2 tog (119 sts).
Row 2	P to last 2 sts, p2 tog (118 sts).
Row 3	K2 tog, k to end (117 sts).
Row 4	P2 tog, p to last 2 sts, p2 tog (115 sts).
Row 5	Rep Row 3 (114 sts).
Row 6	Rep Row 2 (113 sts).
Rows 7–12	Rep Rows 1–6 once (105 sts).
Row 13	Rep Row 1 (103 sts).
Row 14	Rep Row 2 (102 sts). Change to B.
Row 15	Rep Row 3 (101 sts).

Row 16	K2 tog, k to last 2 sts, k2 tog (99 sts). Change to D.
Row 17	Rep Row 3 (98 sts).
Row 18	Rep Row 2 (97 sts).
Rows 19–30	Rep Rows 1–6 twice (81 sts). Change to B.
Row 31	Rep Row 1 (79 sts).
Row 32	K to last 2 sts, k2 tog (78 sts). Change to E.
Rows 33–36	Rep Rows 3–6 once (73 sts).
Rows 37–40	Rep Rows 1–4 once (67 sts).
Row 41	K to end.
Row 42	P to end.
Row 43	K to last 2 sts, k2 tog (66 sts).
Row 44	P to end.
Row 45	K to end.
Row 46	P2 tog, p to end (65 sts). Change to B.
Row 47	K to end.
Row 48	K to end. Change to A.
Row 49	Cast off 3 sts, k to last 2 sts, k2 tog (61 sts).
Row 50	P to last 2 sts, p2 tog (60 sts).
Row 51	Cast off 3 sts, k to end (57 sts).
Row 52	P2 tog, p to last 2 sts, p2 tog (55 sts).
Row 53	Rep Row 51 (52 sts).
Row 54	Rep Row 50 (51 sts).
Rows 55–60	Rep Rows 49–54 once (37 sts).
Rows 61–62	Rep Rows 49–50 once (32 sts). Change to B.

Row 63	Rep Row 49 (28 sts).
Row 64	K to last 2 sts, k2 tog (27 sts). Change to C.
Rows 65–68	Rep Rows 51–54 once (18 sts).
Rows 69–72	Rep Rows 49–52 once (8 sts). Now dec 1 st at each end of every row until all sts are worked off.

LEFT FRONT

With B, cast on 128 sts and work 2 rows in garter-st.

Change to A and work 4in (10cm) in moss-st, dec 1 st at end of second row and at the same edge on every following fourth row (121 sts).

Cont to work exactly as given for the Right Front, reversing shapings.

SLEEVES (MAKE 2)

With C, cast on 18 sts and shape for underarm seam as follows:

Row 1	K twice into first st, k to last st, k twice into last st (20 sts).
Row 2	Cast on 10 sts, p to last st, p twice into last st (31 sts).
Rows 3–12	Rep Rows 1 and 2 five times (96 sts).
Row 13	K twice into first st, k to end (97 sts).
Row 14	P to last st, p twice into last st (98 sts). Change to B.
Row 15	Rep Row 13 (99 sts).
Row 16	K to last st, k twice into last st (100 sts).

Change to D and rep Rows 13 and 14 seven times (114 sts).

Change to B and work 2 rows in garter-st.

Change to A and work 14 rows in St-st.

Change to B and work 2 rows in garter-st.

Change to E and work 14 rows in St-st.

Change to B and dec as follows:

Row 1	K2 tog, k to end (113 sts).
Row 2	K to last 2 sts, k2 tog (112 sts). Change to D.
Row 3	K2 tog, k to end (111 sts).
Row 4	P to last 2 sts, p2 tog (110 sts).
Rows 5–16	Rep Rows 3 and 4 six times (98 sts). Change to B.
Rows 17–18	Rep Rows 1 and 2 once (96 sts). Change to C.
Rows 19–20	Rep Rows 3 and 4 once (94 sts).
Row 21	K2 tog, k to end (93 sts).
Row 22	Cast off 11 sts, p to last 2 sts, p2 tog (81 sts).
Row 23	K2 tog, k to last 2 sts, k2 tog (79 sts).
Row 24	Cast off 10 sts, p to last 2 sts, p2 tog (68 sts).
Rows 25–32	Rep Rows 23 and 24 four times. Cast off rem 16 sts.

CUFFS (MAKE 2)

With B, cast on 60 sts and work 2 rows in garter-st.

Change to A and work 4in (10cm) in moss-st.

Change to B and work 2 rows in garter-st.

With B cast off.

MAKING UP

The garment may be made up on either side: plain or purl, depending on preference.

Pin out pieces, taking extra care not to stretch and making sure the cast-on and cast-off edges measure the same. Press pieces lightly on WS using a warm iron over a damp cloth.

Sew shoulder and side seams of the bodice. Sew sleeve seams and set sleeves into armholes. Join cuff seams to form a circle, then stitch the cuffs to the lower edges of the sleeves.

Find the centre point of the bodice back and the skirt and pin together, making sure both centres match up. stitch the skirt to the bodice, easing in any fullness of either piece and matching the moss-st borders.

Attaching the skirt onto a Petersham band will support the weight of the skirt without dragging, and will prevent the bodice from being pulled out of shape. Stitch the ribbon along the waist seam so that it fits the waist neatly when the fronts are overlapped. Fasten with 2 hooks and eyes or press studs, one on each side at the waistline.

With a 2.5mm hook and A, work 2 rows of dc (sc) along the back neck edge. Darn in ends.

CUDDLESOME CUDDLE SKIRT

The 1950s saw an emphasis on the waist and this classic skirt is no exception to the fashion of the day. The skirt's fullness is given an optional boost with the help of a Vilene lining. It's incredibly simple to knit in stocking stitch, using short rows for shaping at the waist. Use a bright colour as we've done here for extra impact.

DIFFICULTY
+++++

MATERIALS
Sirdar Baby Bamboo DK, 80% bamboo 20% wool, 104yds (95m) per 50g ball, as follows:

22 [23, 23, 24] x 50g in Shade #164 (Perfect Pink)

1 pair 4mm (US #6) needles

1 x 8in (20cm) zip

27½ [29½, 31½, 33½]in (69 [74, 79, 84]cm) x 1in (2.5cm) wide Petersham ribbon (stiff ribbon)

2½yds (2.25m) sew-in Vilene (to line and stiffen skirt — optional)

1 button

SIZING
TO FIT WAIST
26in / 28in / 30in / 32in
(65cm / 70cm / 75cm / 80cm)

ACTUAL FINISHED MEASUREMENTS
Waist
26in / 28in / 30in / 32in
(65cm / 70cm / 75cm / 80cm)

Length (not including waistband)
All sizes: 28in (70cm)

TENSION
24 sts & 28 rows = 4in (10cm) over Stocking stitch.

ABBREVIATIONS
See page 11

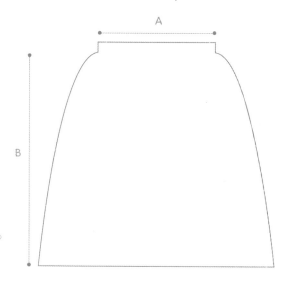

A

B

170

A 13 (14, 15, 16)in
   32.5 (35, 37.5, 40)cm

B 28 (28, 28, 28)in
   70 (70, 70, 70)cm

DIRECTIONS

BACK & FRONT (BOTH ALIKE)
Cast on 240 [246, 252, 258] sts.

Work 4 rows in garter-st.

Commencing with a k row (RS) proceed in St-st until the piece measures 22in (55cm), ending on the WS. If you'd prefer a longer or shorter length, add extra or work fewer rows at this point.

Commence dart shapings as follows:

Row 1 (RS) Sl 1, k37 [38, 39, 40] sts, (sl 1, k1, psso, k2 tog, k76 [78, 80, 82]) twice, sl 1, k1, psso, k2 tog, k38 [39, 40, 41] (234 [240, 246, 252] sts).

Rows 2–4 Work 3 rows without shaping.

Row 5 Sl 1, k 36 [37, 38, 39], (sl 1, k1, psso, k2 tog, k74 [76, 78, 80]) twice, sl 1, k1, psso, k2 tog, k37 [38, 39, 40] (228 [234, 240, 246] sts).

Work 26 [27, 31, 35] rows, dec (as before) in every following 4th row (198 sts).

Work 14 [10, 6, 2] rows, dec (as before) in the next and every other row (156 [168, 180, 192] sts).

Cast off.

WAISTBAND
Cast on 20 sts (all sizes).

Work 4 rows in St-st.

Work buttonhole as follows:

Row 5 (RS) Sl 1, k4, turn.

Working on these 5 sts only, work 6 rows in St-st. Break off yarn. With RS facing, rejoin yarn to rem 15 sts.

Next row K10, turn.

Cont on these 10 sts only, work 6 rows in St-st. Break off yarn.

With RS facing, rejoin yarn to rem 5 sts and work 7 rows in St-st. Do not break off yarn. Working across all 20 sts, sl 1, p to the last st, k1.

Work in St-st until the waistband measures 27½ [29½, 31½, 33½]in (69 [74, 79, 84]cm), ending on WS. Cast off.

MAKING UP
Pin out both pieces to correct dimensions, spray with water and allow to dry. Follow instructions for Lined or Unlined Skirt as below.

Lined skirt only
Cut a paper pattern to correspond with one piece of skirt, allowing ½in (1.5cm) at each side for the seams. Cut out 2 pieces of Vilene to correspond with paper pattern. Sew side edges of Vilene together leaving an 8in (20cm) opening at the top of one side seam. Sew up the side seams of skirt leaving an 8in (20cm) opening at the top of one side seam. Sew zip fastener in position to the fabric at side opening. Place Vilene inside the skirt and sew side opening in position to each side of zip fastener. Sew the Vilene to skirt top just below cast-off edge. Proceed to instructions for 'Lined and Unlined Skirt' below.

Unlined skirt only
Sew up the side seams leaving an 8in (20cm) opening at the top of one side seam. Sew zip fastener in position to the opening. Proceed to instructions for 'Lined and Unlined Skirt' below.

Lined and unlined skirt
Count 13 [14, 15, 16] sts at each side of dart shapings at waist and mark with coloured thread. Fold over to centre of dart and sew together for ½in (1.25cm), remove coloured threads (this forms the unpressed pleats). Flatten out pleats evenly each side of the dart centre and sew along the top to secure.

Fold waistband in half lengthways and with RS facing inwards sew up the short end seams. Turn RS out and pin Petersham ribbon to the inside, slightly stretching the knitting and making sure it sits at the top of the band. Join the bottom of the band, sewing through both sides of fabric just underneath the ribbon leaving approx ½in (1.25cm) open at the bottom.

Cut buttonhole in Petersham ribbon to correspond with skirt buttonhole. Buttonhole stitch round buttonhole. Attach the band to the skirt, splitting the bottom (open) edge of the band fabric so that it straddles the main skirt fabric. Make sure the cast-off end of the waistband is placed to right-hand side of zip and that the buttonhole overhangs the zip by approx 1½in (4cm). Sew each side separately to the front and reverse of the skirt fabric. Sew on button to correspond with buttonhole. Darn in ends.

YARN RESOURCES

All the yarns used in the book are available worldwide.
Some companies distribute out of one specific country,
while others may have many international outlets.
If in doubt, contact them for more details.

YARN COMPANIES

Blouse Front
BC Garn (Worldwide)
Albuen 56A
6000 Kolding, Denmark
info@bcgarn.dk
www.bcgarn.dk

Lumberjacket/Twinset
Cascade Yarns (Worldwide)
PO Box 58168
Tukwila, WA 98138, USA
www.cascadeyarns.com

**Chignon Cap/Book Bag/
Trim Ankle Socks**
Coats Crafts (UK)
Green Lane Mill
Holmfirth
West Yorkshire HD9 2DX, UK
consumer.ccuk@coats.com
www.coatscrafts.co.uk

Westminster Fibers (North America)
8 Shelter Drive
Greer, SC 29560, USA
info@westminsterfibers.com
www.westminsterfibers.com

Double Scarf Jumper
Garnstudio (Worldwide)
Drops Design A/S
Jerikoveien 10 A,
NO–1067 Oslo, Norway
www.garnstudio.com

**Jumper in Stripes of Two Colours
and Two Thicknesses of Wool**
Excelana (Worldwide)
Fibre Harvest
John Arbon Textiles
PO Box 8 Lynton
North Devon EX35 6WY, UK
Tel: 01598 752490
juliet@jarbon.com
www.jarbon.com

Susan Crawford Vintage (Retail)
The Studio
Rear of Balmoral Drive
Southport PR9 8QE, UK
Tel: 01704 320052
sales@susancrawfordvintage.com
www.susancrawfordvintage.com

Half Blouse
Fyberspates (Worldwide)
Unit 1 Oxleaze Farm Workshops
Broughton Poggs
Filkins, Lechlade
Gloucester GL7 3RB, UK
Tel: 01367 850880
fyberspates@btinternet.com
www.fyberspates.co.uk

Headscarf/Attractive Skull Cap
Handmaiden (Lace Silk) (Worldwide)
Canada
handmaiden@fleeceartist.com
www.handmaiden.ca

Charming Dress
Holst Garn (Worldwide)
Denmark
holstgarn@email.dk
www.holstgarn.dk

Two-Colour Spot Jersey
Jamieson's (UK and Europe)
Sandness Industrial Estate
Sandness
Shetland Islands ZE2 9PL, UK
Tel: 01595 693114
lerwick@jamiesonsofshetland.co.uk
www.jamiesonsofshetland.co.uk

Jamieson's (USA and Canada)
Simply Shetland
18375 Olympic Avenue South
Seattle, WA 98188, USA
info@simplyshetland.net
www.simplyshetland.net

**Housecoat/Spiral Pattern Jumper/
Waistcoat/Book Bag**
Jamieson & Smith (Worldwide)
Shetland Wool Brokers
90 North Road
Lerwick, Shetland Islands, UK
Tel: 01595 693579
sales@shetlandwoolbrokers.co.uk
www.shetlandwoolbrokers.co.uk

**Man's Cardigan/Man's Scarf and
Gloves**
Juno Fibre Arts (Worldwide)
Devon, UK
info@junofibrearts.com
www.junofibrearts.com

Attractive Jumper with Slanting Yoke
Koigu Wool Designs (Worldwide)
Box 158
Chatsworth
ON, N0H 1G0, Canada
taiu@koigu.com
www.koigu.com

Polo Mode Hats
Orkney Angora (Worldwide), UK
Isle of Sanday
Orkney KW17 2AZ, UK
Tel: 08157 600421
info@orkneyangora.co.uk
www.orkneyangora.co.uk

Knitted Collar
Rico Design (Worldwide)
Industriestrasse 19–23
33034 Brakel, Germany
info@ricò-design.de
www.rico-design.de

Polo Mode Hats/Tricolour Pullover
Rowan (UK)
Green Lane Mill
Holmfirth
West Yorkshire HD9 2DX, UK
Tel: 01484 681881
mail@knitrowan.com
www.knitrowan.com

Westminster Fibers (North America)
8 Shelter Drive
Greer, SC 29560, USA
info@westminsterfibers.com
www.westminsterfibers.com

Cuddlesome Cuddle Skirt
Sirdar Spinning (Worldwide)
Flanshaw Lane
Wakefield
West Yorkshire WF2 9ND, UK
enquiries@sirdar.co.uk
www.sirdar.co.uk

Blouse with a Round Yoke
Thomas B. Ramsden & Co (UK)
Netherfield Road
Guiseley
Leeds LS20 9PD, UK
Tel: 01943 872264
enquiries@tbramsden.co.uk
www.tbramsden.co.uk

www.handknitting.com
8250 Henry's Road, Jackson
Wyoming, 83001, USA
laurel@handknitting.com
www.handknitting.com

Tuck-In Surplice
Rohrspatz & Wollmeise (Worldwide)
Germany
www.rohrspatzundwollmeise.de

The Loopy Ewe
2720 Council Tree Avenue, Suite 255
Fort Collins
Colorado, 80525, USA
support@theloopyewe.com
www.theloopyewe.com

Deramores (online sales)
Tel: 0800 4880708
www.deramores.co.uk

Loop
15 Camden Passage
Islington
London N1 8EA, UK
info@loopknitting.com
www.loopknittingshop.com

PICTURE CREDITS

Every effort has been made to contact the copyright
holders of the original patterns, but should there be
any errors or omissions, Laurence King Publishing would
be pleased to correct them in any subsequent printing
of this publication.

Attractive Skull Cap for Casual Wear, Knitted Collar, Headscarf, Man's
Scarf and Gloves in a Four-Colour Pattern, Twelve Polo Mode Hats,
Trim Ankle Socks, Attractive Jumper with Slanting Yoke in Cable Stitch,
Blouse Front, Jumper in Stripes of Two Colours and Two Thicknesses
of Wool, Man's Cardigan, A Twinset in Simple Stitches (a Duet in
Knitting), Two-Colour Spot Jersey, A Waistcoat in Cloque Pattern,
Charming Dress and Fashionable Housecoat all © IPC+ Syndication.

Chignon Cap © 1955 Coats & Clark Inc.
Reproduced with permission of Coats & Clark Inc.

Book Bag © 1935 Coats & Clark Inc.
Reproduced with permission of Coats & Clark Inc.

Blouse with a Round Yoke reproduced with permission
of Thomas B Ramsden & Co (Bradford) Limited.

Lady's Jumper with a Double Scarf Collar and Spiral Pattern
Jumper reproduced with permission of Coats plc.

Tricolour Pullover and Tuck-in Surplice reproduced
with permission of Hearst Communication Inc.

Cuddlesome Cuddle Skirt reproduced with permission
of Sirdar Spinning Ltd.

All photography by Simon Pask except pages 13–15, 25–26, 29, 31, 89
& 92; photography by Marine Malak and Alex Madjitey.

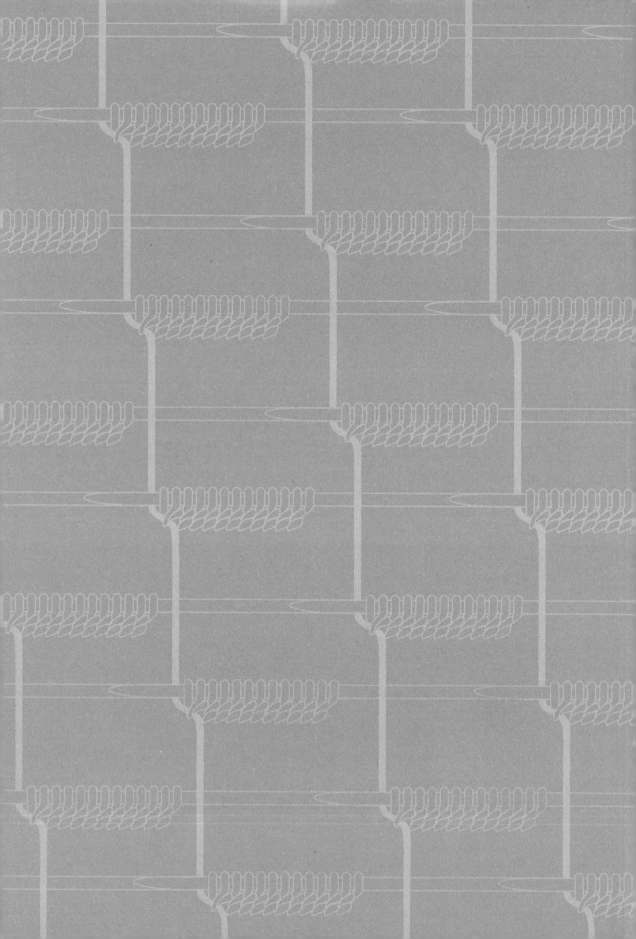